CLUTTON-BROCK, Arth

Essays on art. Freeport, N.Y., Books for
Libraries Pr. [1968]
143p. (Essays index reprint series)
Reprinted from the Times literary supplement.
Reprint. 1st pub. 1919.

1. Art - Addresses, essays, lectures I.
tc.

F5808 Z

ESSAYS ON ART

ESSAYS ON ART

BY

A. CLUTTON-BROCK

Essay Index Reprint Series

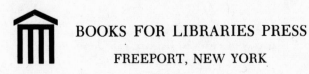

BOOKS FOR LIBRARIES PRESS

FREEPORT, NEW YORK

First Published 1919
Reprinted 1968

Essay Index Reprint Series

LIBRARY OF CONGRESS CATALOG CARD NUMBER:

68-22906

PRINTED IN THE UNITED STATES OF AMERICA

PREFACE

THESE essays, reprinted from the *Times Literary Supplement* with a few additions and corrections, are not all entirely or directly concerned with art; but even the last one—Waste or Creation?—does bear on the question, How are we to improve the art of our own time? After years of criticism I am more interested in this question than in any other that concerns the arts. Whistler said that we could not improve it; the best we could do for it was not to think about it. I have discussed that opinion, as also the contrary opinion of Tolstoy, and the truth that seems to me to lie between them. If these essays have any unity, it is given to them by my belief that art, like other human activities, is subject to the will of man. We cannot cause men of artistic genius to be born; but we can provide a public, namely, ourselves, for the artist, who will encourage him to be an

b   v

artist, to do his best, not his worst. I believe
that the quality of art in any age depends, not
upon the presence or absence of individuals of
genius, but upon the attitude of the public
towards art.

Because of the decline of all the arts, especially the arts of use, which began at the end of
the eighteenth century and has continued up
to our own time, we are more interested in art
than any people of the past, with the interest
of a sick man in health. To say that this
interest must be futile or mischievous is to
deny the will of man in one of the chief of
human activities; but it often is denied by
those who do not understand how it can be
applied to art. We cannot make artists
directly; no government office can determine
their training; still less can any critic tell
them how they ought to practise their art.
But we can all aim at a state of society in
which they will be encouraged to do their best,
and at a state of mind in which we ourselves
shall learn to know good from bad and to
prefer the good. At present we have neither
the state of society nor the state of mind; and
we càn attain to both not by connoisseurship,

Preface

not by an anxiety to like the right thing or at
least to buy it, but by learning the difference
between good and bad workmanship and design in objects of use. Anyone can do that,
and can resolve to pay a fair price for good
workmanship and design; and only so will the
arts of use, and all the arts, revive again. For
where the public has no sense of design in the
arts of use, it will have none in the "fine arts."
To aim at connoisseurship when you do not
know a good table or chair from a bad one is
to attempt flying before you can walk. So, I
think, professors of art at Oxford or Cambridge
should be chosen, not so much for their knowledge of Greek sculpture, as for their success in
furnishing their own houses. What can they
know about Greek sculpture if their own
drawing-rooms are hideous? I believe that
the notorious fallibility of many experts is
caused by the fact that they concern themselves with the fine arts before they have had
any training in the arts of use. So, if we are
to have a school of art at Oxford or Cambridge,
it should put this question to every pupil: If
you had to build and furnish a house of your
own, how would you set about it? And it

should train its pupils to give a rational answer to that question. So we might get a public knowing the difference between good and bad in objects of use, valuing the good, and ready to pay a fair price for it.

At present we have no such public. A liberal education should teach the difference between good and bad in things of use, including buildings. Oxford and Cambridge profess to give a liberal education; but you have only to look at their modern buildings to see that their teachers themselves do not know a good building from a bad one. They, like all the rest of us, think that taste in art is an irrational mystery; they trust in the expert and usually in the wrong one, as the ignorant and superstitious trust in the wrong priest. For as religion is merely mischievous unless it is tested in matters of conduct, so taste is mere pedantry or frivolity unless it is tested on things of use. These have their sense or nonsense, their righteousness or unrighteousness, which anyone can learn to see for himself, and, until he has learned, he will be at the mercy of charlatans.

I have written all these essays as a member

Preface

of the public, as one who has to find a right attitude towards art so that the arts may flourish again. The critic is sure to be a charlatan or a prig, unless he is to himself not a pseudo-artist expounding the mysteries of art and telling artists how to practise them, but simply one of the public with a natural and human interest in art. But one of these essays is a defence of criticism, and I will not repeat it here.

A. CLUTTON-BROCK

July 30, 1919
FARNCOMBE, SURREY

CONTENTS

	PAGE
"The Adoration of the Magi" . .	1
Leonardo da Vinci	13
The Pompadour in Art . . .	27
An Unpopular Master . . .	37
A Defence of Criticism . . .	48
The Artist and his Audience . .	58
Wilfulness and Wisdom . . .	74
"The Magic Flute"	86
Process or Person?	97
The Artist and the Tradesman . .	110
Professionalism in Art . . .	120
Waste or Creation?	132

ESSAYS ON ART

"The Adoration of the Magi" ᴓ ᴓ

THERE is one beauty of nature and
another of art, and many attempts have
been made to explain the difference between
them. Signor Croce's theory, now much in
favour, is that nature provides only the raw
material for art. The beginning of the artistic
process is the perception of beauty in nature;
but an artist does not see beauty as he sees a
cow. It is his own mind that imposes on the
chaos of nature an order, a relation, which is
beauty. All men have the faculty, in some
degree, of imposing this order; the artist only
does it more completely than other men, and
he owes his power of execution to that. He
can make the beauty which he has perceived
because he has perceived it clearly; and this
perceiving is part of the making.

The defect of this theory is that it ends
by denying that very difference between the

beauty of nature and the beauty of art which
it sets out to explain. If the artist makes the
beauty of nature in perceiving it, if it is produced by the action of his own mind upon the
chaos of reality, then it is the very same beauty
that appears in his art; and if, to us, the
beauty of his art seems different from the
beauty of nature, as we perceive it, it is only
because we have not ourselves seen the beauty
of nature as completely as he has, we have not
reduced chaos so thoroughly to order. It is a
difference not of kind, but of degree; for the
artist himself there is no difference even of
degree. What he makes he sees, and what he
sees he makes. All beauty is artistic, and to
speak of natural beauty is to make a false
distinction.

Yet it is a distinction that we remain constantly aware of. In spite of Signor Croce
and all the subtlety and partial truth of his
theory, we do not believe that we make beauty
when we see it, or that the artist makes it
when he sees it. Nor do we believe that that
beauty which he makes is of the same nature
as that which he has perceived in reality.
Rather he, like us, values the beauty which he
perceives in reality because he knows that he
has not made it. It is something, independent

of himself, to which his own mind makes
answer: that answer is his art; it is the
passionate value expressed in it which gives
beauty to his art. If he knew that the beauty
he perceives was a product of his own mind, he
could not value it so; if he held Signor Croce's
theory, he would cease to be an artist.

And, in fact, those who act on his theory
do cease to be artists. Nothing kills art so
certainly as the effort to produce a beauty of
the same kind as that which is perceived in
nature. In the beauty of nature, as we perceive it, there is a perfection of workmanship
which is perfection because there is no workmanship. Natural things are not made, but
born; works of art are made. There is the
essential difference between them and between
their beauties. If a work of art tries to have
the finish of a thing born, not made, if a piece
of enamel apes the gloss of a butterfly's wing,
it misses the peculiar beauty of art and is but
an inadequate imitation of the beauty of nature.
That beauty of the butterfly's wing, which the
artist like all of us perceives, is of a different
kind from any beauty he can make; and if he
is an artist he knows it and does not try to
make it. But all the arts, even those which
are not themselves imitative, are always being

perverted by the attempt to imitate the finish of nature. There is a vanity of craftsmanship in Louis Quinze furniture, in the later Chinese porcelain, in modern jewelry, no less than in Dutch painting, which is the death of art. All great works of art show an effort, a roughness, an inadequacy of craftsmanship, which is the essence of their beauty and distinguishes it from the beauty of nature. As soon as men cease to understand this and despise this effort and roughness and inadequacy, they demand from art the beauty of nature and get something which is mostly dead nature, not living art.

We can best understand the difference between the two kinds of beauty if we consider how beauty steals into language, that art which we all practise more or less and in which it is difficult, if not impossible, to imitate the finish of natural beauty. There is no beauty whatever in sentences like " Trespassers will be prosecuted " or " Pass the mustard," because they say exactly and completely all that they have to say. There is beauty in sentences like " The bright day is done, And we are for the dark," or " After life's fitful fever he sleeps well," because in them, although they seem quite simple, the poet is trying to say a thousand times more than he can say. It is the effort to do something beyond the power of words that brings beauty into them. That is the very nature of the beauty of art, which distinguishes it from the beauty of nature; it is always produced by the effort to accomplish the impossible, and what the artist knows to be impossible. Whenever that effort ceases, whenever the artist sets himself a task that he can accomplish, a task of mere skill, then he ceases to be an artist, because he no longer experiences reality in the manner necessary to an artist. The great poet is aware of some excellence in reality so intensely that it is to him beauty; for all excellence when we are intensely aware of it is beauty to us. There is that truth in Croce's theory. Our perception of beauty does depend upon the intensity of our perception of excellence. But that intensity of perception remains perception, and does not make what it perceives. That the poet and every artist knows; and his art is not merely an extension of the process of perception, but an attempt to express his own value for that excellence which he has perceived as beauty. It is an answer to that beauty, a worship of it, and is itself beautiful because it makes no effort to compete with it.

Thus in the beauty of art there is always value and wonder, always a reference to another beauty different in kind from itself; and we too, if we are to see the beauty of art, must share the same value and wonder. To enter that Kingdom of Heaven we must become little children as the artist himself does. Art is the expression of a certain attitude towards reality, an attitude of wonder and value, a recognition of something greater than man; and where that recognition is not, art dies. In a society valuing only itself, believing that it can make a heaven of itself out of its own skill and knowledge and wisdom, the difference between the beauty of nature and the beauty of art is no longer seen, and art loses all its own beauty. The surest sign of corruption and death in a society is where men and women see the best life as a life without wonder or effort or failure, where labour is hidden underground so that a few may seem to live in Paradise; where there is perfect finish of all things, human beings no less than their clothes and furniture and buildings and pictures; where the ideal is the lady so perfectly turned out that any activity whatever would mar her perfection. In such societies the artist becomes a slave. He too must produce work that does

not seem to be work. He must express no
wonder or value for patrons who would be
ashamed to feel either. What he makes must
seem to be born and not made, so that it may
fit a world which pretends to be a born Paradise populated by cynical angels who own
allegiance to no god. In such a world art
means, beauty means, the concealment of effort,
the pretence that it does not exist; and that
pretence is the end of art and beauty in all
things made by man. There is a close connexion between the idea of life expressed in
Aristotle's ideal man and the later Greek
sculpture. The aim of that sculpture, as of
his ideal man, was proud and effortless perfection. Both dread the confession of failure
above all things — and both are dull. In
Aristotle's age art had started upon a long
decline, which ended only when the pretence
of perfection was killed, both in art and in life,
by Christianity. Then the real beauty of art,
the beauty of value and wonder, superseded
the wearisome imitation of natural beauty;
and it is only lately that we have learnt again
to prefer the real beauty to the false.

Men must free themselves from the contempt
of effort and the desire to conceal it, they must
be content with the perpetual, passionate

failure of art, before they can see its beauty
or demand that beauty from the artist.   When
they themselves become like little children,
then they see that the greatest artists, in all
their seeming triumphs, are like little children
too.   For in Michelangelo and Beethoven it
is not the arrogant, the accomplished, the
magnificent, that moves us.   They are great
men to us; but they achieved beauty because
in their effort to achieve it they were little
children to themselves.   They impose awe on
us, but it is their own awe that they impose.
It is not their achievement that makes beauty,
but their effort, always confessing its own
failure; and in that confession is the beauty of
art.   That is 'why it moves and frees us; for it
frees us from our pretence that we are what
we would be, it carries us out of our own
egotism into the wonder and value of the artist
himself.

Consider the beauty of a tune.   Music itself
is the best means which man has found for
confessing that he cannot say what he would
say; and it is more purely and rapturously
beauty than any other form of art.   A tune is
the very silencing of speech, and in the greatest
tunes there is always the hush of wonder: they
seem to tell us to be silent and listen, not to

what the musician has to say, but to what he
cannot say. The very beauty of a tune is in
its reference to something beyond all expression, and in its perfection it speaks of a perfection not its own. Pater said that all art tries
to attain to the condition of music. That is
true in a sense different from what he meant.
Art is always most completely art when it
makes music's confession of the ineffable; then
it comes nearest to the beauty of music. But
when it is no longer a forlorn hope, when it is
able to say what it wishes to say with calm
assurance, then it has ceased to be art and
become a game of skill.

Often the great artist is imperious, impatient,
full of certainties; but his certainty is not of
himself; and he is impatient of the failure to
recognize, not himself, but what he recognizes.
Michelangelo, Beethoven, Tintoret, would snap
a critic's head off if he did not see what they
were trying to do. They may seem sometimes
to be arrogant in the mere display of power,
yet their beauty lies in the sudden change from
arrogance to humility. The arrogance itself
bows down and worships; the very muscle and
material force obey a spirit not their own.
They are lion-tamers, and they themselves are
the lions; out of the strong comes forth sweet-

ness, and it is all the sweeter for the strength
that is poured into it and subdued by it.
What is the difference, as of different worlds,
between Rubens at his best and Tintoret at his
best? This: that Rubens always seems to be
uplifted by his own power, whereas Tintoret
has most power when he forgets it in wonder.
When he bows down all his turbulence in
worship, then he is most strong. Rubens, in
the "Descent from the Cross," is still the
supreme drawing-master; and painters flocking
to him for lessons pay homage to him. But,
in his "Crucifixion," it is Tintoret himself who
pays homage, and we forget the master in the
theme. We may say of Rubens's art, in a new
sense, "C'est magnifique, mais ce n'est pas la
guerre." The greatest art is not magnificent,
but it is war, desperate and without trappings,
a war in which victory comes through the
confession of defeat.

Man, if he tries to be a god in his art, makes
a fool of himself. He becomes like God, he
makes beauty like God, when he is too much
aware of God to be aware of himself. Then
only does he not set himself too easy a task,
for then he does not make his theme so that he
may accomplish it; it is forced upon him by
his awareness of God, by his wonder and value

for an excellence not his own. So in all the
beauty of art there is a humility not only of
conception, but also of execution, which is mere
failure and ugliness to those who expect to find
in art the beauty and finish of nature, who
expect it to be born, not made. They are
always disappointed by the greatest works of
art, by their inadequacy and strain and labour.
They look for a proof of what man can do and
find a confession of what he cannot do ; but
that confession, made sincerely and passionately, is beauty. There is also a serenity in
the beauty of art, but it is the serenity of self-
surrender, not of self-satisfaction, of the saint,
not of the lady of fashion. And all the accomplishment of great art, its infinite superiority
in mere skill over the work of the merely
skilful, comes from the incessant effort of the
artist to do more than he can. By that he is
trained ; by that his work is distinguished from
the mere exclamation of wonder. He is not
content to applaud ; he must also worship, and
make his offerings in his worship ; and they
are the best he can do. It was not only the
shepherds who came to the birth of Christ ;
the wise men came also and brought their
treasures with them. And the art of mankind
is the offering of its wise men, it is the adora-

tion of the Magi, who are one with the simplest in their worship—

> Wise men, all ways of knowledge past,
> To the Shepherd's wonder come at last.

But they do not lose their wisdom in their wonder. When it passes into wonder, when all the knowledge and skill and passion of mankind are poured into the acknowledgment of something greater than themselves, then that acknowledgment is art, and it has a beauty which may be envied by the natural beauty of God Himself.

Leonardo da Vinci ✑ ✑ ✑ ✑

LEONARDO DA VINCI is one of the most famous men in history—as a man more famous than Michelangelo or Shakespeare or Mozart—because posterity has elected him the member for the Renaissance. Most great artists live in what they did, and by that we know them; but what Leonardo did gets much of its life from what he was, or rather from what he is to us. Of all great men he is the most representative; we cannot think of him as a mere individual, eating and drinking, living and competing, on equal terms with other men. We see him magnified by his own legend from the first, with people standing aside to watch and whisper as he passed through the streets of Florence or Milan. "There he goes to paint the Last Supper," they said to each other; and we think of it as already the most famous picture in the world before it was begun. Every one knew that he had the most famous picture in his brain, that he was born

13

to paint it, to initiate the High Renaissance; from Giotto onwards all the painters had been preparing for that, Florence herself had been preparing for it. It makes no difference that for centuries it has been a shadow on the wall; it is still the most famous painting in the world because it is the masterpiece of Leonardo. There was a fate against the survival of his masterpieces, but he has survived them and they are remembered because of him. We accept him for himself, like the people of his own time, who, when he said he could perform impossibilities, believed him. To them he meant the new age which could do anything, and still to us he means the infinite capacities of man. He is the Adam awakened whom Michelangelo only painted; and, if he accomplished but little, we believe in him, as in mankind, for his promise. If he did not fulfil it, neither has mankind; but he believed that all things could be done and lived a great life in that faith.

Another Florentine almost equals him in renown. Men watched and whispered when Dante passed through the streets of Florence; but Dante lives in his achievement, Leonardo in himself. Dante means to us an individual soul quivering through a system, a creed, in-

Leonardo da Vinci

herited from the past. Leonardo is a spirit unstraitened; not consenting to any past nor rebelling against it, but newborn with a newborn universe around it, seeing it without memories or superstitions, without inherited fears or pieties, yet without impiety or irreverence. He is not an iconoclast, since for him there are no images to be broken; whatever he sees is not an image but itself, to be accepted or rejected by himself; what he would do he does without the help or hindrance of tradition. In art and in science he means the same thing, not a rebirth of any past, as the word Renaissance seems to imply, but freedom from all the past, life utterly in the present. He is concerned not with what has been thought, or said, or done, but with his own immediate relation to all things, with what he sees and feels and discovers. Authority is nothing to him, whether of Galen or of St. Thomas, of Greek or mediæval art. In science he looks at the fact, in art at the object; nor will he allow either to be hidden from him by the achievements of the dead. Giotto had struck the first blow for freedom when he allowed the theme to dictate the picture; Leonardo allowed the object to dictate the drawing. To him the fact itself is sacred, and man fulfils himself in his own immediate relation to fact.

All those who react and rebel against the Renaissance have an easy case against its great representative. What did he do in thought compared with St. Thomas, or in art compared with the builders of Chartres or Bourges? He filled notebooks with sketches and conjectures; he modelled a statue that was never cast; he painted a fresco on a wall, and with a medium so unsuited to fresco that it was a ruin in a few years. Even in his own day there was a doubt about him; it is expressed in the young Michelangelo's sudden taunt that he could not cast the statue he had modelled. Michelangelo was one of those who see in life always the great task to be performed and who judge a man by his performance; to him Leonardo was a dilettante, a talker; he made monuments, but Leonardo remains his own monument, a prophecy of what man shall be when he comes into his kingdom. With him, we must confess, it is more promise than performance; he could paint "The Last Supper" because it means the future; he could never, in good faith, have painted "The Last Judgment," for that means a judgment on the past, and to him the past is nothing; to him man, in the

Leonardo da Vinci

future, is the judge, master, enjoyer of his own
fate. Compared with his, Michelangelo's mind
was still mediæval, his reproach the reproach
of one who cares for doing more than for
being, and certainly Michelangelo did a thousand times more; but from his own day to ours
the world has not judged Leonardo by his
achievement. As Johnson had his Boswell so
he has had his legend; he means to us not
books or pictures, but himself. In his own
day kings bid for him as if he were a work
of art; and he died magnificently in France,
making nothing but foretelling a race of men
not yet fulfilled.

Before Francis Bacon, before Velasquez or
Manet, he prophesied not merely the new artist
or the new man of science, but the new man
who is to free himself from his inheritance and
to see, feel, think, and act in all things with
the spontaneity of God. That is why he is a
legendary hero to us, with a legend that is not
in the past but in the future. For his prophecy
is still far from fulfilment; and the very science
that he initiated tells us how hard it is for
man to free himself from his inheritance. It
seems strange to us that Leonardo sang hymns
to causation as if to God. In its will was his
peace and his freedom.

O marvellous necessity, thou with supreme reason constrainest all efforts to be the direct result of their causes, and by a supreme and irrevocable law every natural action obeys thee by the shortest possible process.

Who would believe that so small a space could contain the images of all the universe? O mighty process, what talent can avail to penetrate a nature such as thine? What tongue will it be that can unfold so great a wonder? Verily none. This it is that guides the human discourse to the considering of divine things.[1]

To Leonardo causation meant the escape from caprice; it meant a secure relation between man and all things, in which man would gain power by knowledge, in which every increase of knowledge would reveal to him more and more of the supreme reason. There was no chain for him in cause and effect, no unthinking of the will of man. Rather by knowledge man would discover his own will and know that it was the universal will. So man must never be afraid of knowledge. "The eye is the window of the soul." Like Whitman he tells us always to look with the eye, and so to confound the wisdom of ages. There is in every man's vision the power of relating himself

[1] The sayings of Leonardo quoted in this article are taken from *Leonardo da Vinci's Notebooks*, by E. M'Curdy. (Duckworth, 1906.)

Leonardo da Vinci

now and directly to reality by knowledge; and
in knowing other things he knows himself. By
knowledge man changes what seemed to be a
compulsion into a harmony; he gives up his
own caprice for the universal will.

That is the religion of Leonardo, in art as
in science. For him the artist also must relate
himself directly to the visible world, in which
is the only inspiration; to accept any formula
is to see with dead men's eyes. That has been
said again and again by artists, but not with
Leonardo's mystical and philosophical con-
viction. He knew that it is vain to study
Nature unless she is to you a goddess or a god;
you can learn nothing from reality unless you
adore it, and in adoring it he found his freedom.
How different is this doctrine from that with
which, after centuries of scientific advance, we
intimidate ourselves. We are threatened by
a creed far more enslaving than that of the
Middle Ages. If the Middle Ages turned to
the past to learn what they were to think or
to do, we turn to the past to learn what we
are. They may have feared the new; but we
say that there is no new, nothing but some
combination or variation of the old. Causation is to us a chain that binds us to the past,
but to Leonardo it was freedom; and so he

prophesies a freedom that we may attain to not by denying facts or making myths, but by discovering what he hinted—that causation itself is not compulsion but will, and our will if, by knowledge, we make it ours.

No one before him had been so much in love with reality, whatever it may be. He was called a sceptic, but it was only that he preferred reality itself to any tales about it; and his religion, his worship, was the search for the very fact. This, because he was both artist and man of science, he carried further than anyone else, pursuing it with all his faculties. In his drawings there is the beauty not of his character, but of the character of what he draws; he does not make a design, but finds it. That beauty proves him a Florentine— Dürer himself falls short of it—but it is the beauty of the thing itself, discovered and insisted upon with the passion of a lover. He draws animals, trees, flowers, as Correggio draws Antiope or Io; and it is only in his drawings now that he speaks clearly to us. The "Mona Lisa" is well enough, but another hand might have executed the painting of it. It owes its popular fame to the smile about which it is so easy to write finely; but in the drawings we see the experiencing passion of

Leonardo da Vinci

Leonardo himself, we see him feeling, as in the notebooks we see him thinking. There is the eagerness of discovery at which so often he stopped short, turning away from a task to further discovery, living always in the moment, taking no thought either for the morrow or for yesterday, unable to attend to any business, even the business of the artist, seeing life not as a struggle or a duty, but as an adventure of all the senses and all the faculties. He is, even with his pencil, the greatest talker in the world, but without egotism, talking always of what he sees, satisfying himself not with the common appetites and passions of men, but with his one supreme passion for reality. If Michelangelo thought him a dilettante, there must have been in his taunt some envy of Leonardo's freedom.

Yet once at least Leonardo did achieve, and something we should never have expected from his drawings. "The Last Supper" is but a shadow on the wall, yet still we can see its greatness, which is the greatness of pure design, of Giotto, Masaccio, Piero della Francesa. Goethe and others have found all kinds of psychological subtleties in it, meanings in every gesture; but what we see now is only space, grandeur, a supreme moment expressed in the relation of all the forms. The pure music of the painting remains when the drama is almost obliterated; and it proves that Leonardo, when he chose, could withdraw himself from the delight of hand-to-mouth experience into a vision of his own, that he had the reserve and the creative power of the earlier masters and of that austere, laborious youth who taunted him. If it were not for "The Last Supper" we might doubt whether he could go further in art than the vivid sketch of "The Magi"; but "The Last Supper" tells us how great his passion for reality must have been, since it could distract him from the making of such masterpieces.

That passion for reality itself made him cold to other passions. We know Michelangelo and Beethoven as men in some respects very like other men. They were anxious, fretful, full of affections and grievances, and much concerned with their relations. Leonardo is like Melchizedek, not only by the accident of birth, for he was a natural son, but by choice. He never married, he never had a home; there is no evidence that he was ever tied to any man or woman by his affections; yet it would be stupid to call him cold, for his one grand passion absorbed him. Monks suspected him, but in his heart he was celibate like the great monkish saints, celibate not by vows but by

Leonardo da Vinci

preoccupation. It is clear that from youth to age life had no cumulative power over him; as we should say in our prosaic language, he never settled down, for he let things happen to him and valued the very happening. He was always like a strange, wonderful creature from another planet, taking notes with unstaled delight but never losing his heart to any particular. Sex itself seems hardly to exist for him, or at least for his mind. Often the people in his drawings are of no sex. Rembrandt draws every one, Leonardo no one, as if he were his own relation. Women and youths were as much a subject of his impassioned curiosity as flowers, and no more. He is always the spectator, but a spectator who can exercise every faculty of the human mind and every passion in contemplation; he is the nearest that any man has ever come to Aristotle's Supreme Being.

But we must not suppose that he went solemnly through life living up to his own story, that he was mysterious in manner or in any respect like a charlatan. Rather, he lived always in the moment and overcame mankind by his spontaneity. He had the charm of the real man of genius, not the reserve of the false one. The famous statement of what he could

do, which he made to Ludovico Sforza, is not a
mere boast but an expression of his eagerness
to do it. These engines of war were splendid
toys to him, and all his life he enjoyed making
toys and seeing men wonder at them. His
delight was to do things for the first time like
a child, and then not to do them again.
Again and again he cries out against authority
and in favour of discovery. "Whoever in dis-
cussion adduces authority," he says, "uses not
intellect but rather memory"; and, anticipat-
ing Milton, he observes that all our knowledge
originates in opinions. Perhaps some one had
rebuked him for having too many opinions.
We can be sure that he chafed against dull,
cautious, safe men who wished for results. He
himself cared nothing for them; it was enough
for him to know what might be done, without
doing it. He was so sure of his insight that
he did not care to put it to the test of action;
that was for slower men, whether artists or
men of science. His notebooks were enough
for him.

In spite of the notebooks and the sketches,
we know less about the man Leonardo than
about the man Shakespeare. Here and there
he makes a remark with some personal con-
viction or experience in it. "Intellectual

passion," he says, "drives out sensuality." In him it had driven out or sublimated all the sensual part of character. We cannot touch or see or hear him in anything he says or draws. The passion is there, but it is too much concerned with universals to be of like nature with our own passions. He seems to be speaking to himself as if he had forgotten the whole audience of mankind, but in what he says he ignores the personal part of himself; he is most passionate when most impersonal. "To the ambitious, whom neither the boon of life nor the beauty of the world suffices to content, it comes as a penance that life with them is squandered and that they possess neither the benefits nor the beauty of the world." That might be a platitude said by some one else; but we know that in it Leonardo expresses his faith. The boon of life, the beauty of the world, were enough for him without ambition, without even further affections. He left father and mother and wealth, and even achievement, to follow them; and he left all those not out of coldness, or fear, or idleness, but because his own passion drew him away. No cold man could have said, "Where there is most power of feeling, there of martyrs is the greatest martyr." It is difficult for us northerners to understand the intellectual passion of the South, to see even that it is passion; most difficult of all for us to see that in men like Leonardo the passion for beauty itself is intellectual. We, with our romanticism, our sense of exile, can never find that identity which he found between beauty and reality. "This benign nature so provides that all over the world you find something to imitate." To us imitation means prose, to him it meant poetry; science itself meant poetry, and illusion was the only ugliness. "Nature never breaks her own law." It is we who try to find freedom in lawlessness, which is ignorance, ugliness, illusion. "Falsehood is so utterly vile that, though it should praise the great works of God, it offends against His divinity." There is Leonardo's religion; and if still it is too cold for us, it is because we have not his pure spiritual fire in ourselves.

The Pompadour in Art ❧ ❧ ❧

IT is an important fact in the history of the
arts for the last century or more that in
England and America, if not elsewhere, the
chief interest in all the arts, including literature, has been taken by women rather than
by men. In the great ages of art it was not
so. Women, so far as we can tell, had little
to do with the art of Greece in the fifth century
or with the art of the Middle Ages. There
were female patrons of art at the Renaissance,
but they were exceptions subject to the pre-
vailing masculine taste. Art was and remained
a proper interest of men up to the eighteenth
century. Women first began to control it and
to affect its character at the mistress-ridden
Court of Louis XV. But in the nineteenth
century men began to think they were too busy
to concern themselves with the arts. Men of
power, when they were not working, needed
to take exercise and left it to their wives to
patronize the arts. And so the notion grew

27

that art was a feminine concern, and even artists were pets for women. The great man, especially in America, liked his wife to have every luxury. The exquisite life she led was itself a proof of his success; and she was for him a living work of art, able to live so because of the abundance of his strength. In her, that strength passed into ornament and became beautiful; she was a friendly, faithful Delilah to his Samson, a Delilah who did not shear his locks. And so he came to think of art itself as being in its nature feminine if not effeminate, as a luxury and ornament of life, as everything, in fact, except a means of expression for himself and other men.

This female control of art began, as I have said, at the mistress-ridden Court of Louis XV, and it has unfortunately kept the stamp of its origin. At that Court art, to suit the tastes of the Pompadour and the Du Barri, became consciously frivolous, became almost a part of the toilet. The artist was the slave of the mistress, and seems to have enjoyed his chains. In this slavery he did produce something charming; he did invest that narrow and artificial Heaven of the Court with some of the infinite beauty and music of a real Heaven. But out of this refined harem art there has

sprung a harem art of the whole world which
has infested the homes even of perfectly respectable ladies ever since. All over Europe the
ideals of applied art have remained the ideals
of the Pompadour ; and only by a stern and conscious effort have either women or men been able
to escape from them. Everywhere there has
spread a strange disease of romantic snobbery,
the sufferers from which, in their efforts at
æsthetic expression, always pretend to be what
they are not. Excellent mothers óf families,
in their furniture and sometimes even in their
clothes, pretend to be King's mistresses. Of
course, if this pretence were put into words and
so presented to their consciousness, they would
be indignant. It has for them no connexion with
conduct ; it is purely æsthetic, but art means to
them make-believe, the make-believe that they
live an entirely frivolous life of pleasure provided
for them by masculine power and devotion.

Yet these ladies know that they have not the
revenues of the Pompadour ; they must have
their art, their make-believe, as cheap as
possible ; and it has been one of the triumphs
of modern industry to provide them with cheap
imitations of the luxury of the Pompadour.
Hence the machine-made frivolities of the most
respectable homes, the hair-brushes with backs

of stamped silver, the scent-bottles of imitation cut-glass, the draperies with printed rose-buds on them, the general artificial-floweriness and flimsiness and superfluity of naughtiness of our domestic art. It expresses a feminine romance to which the male indulgently consents, as if he were really the voluptuous monarch whose mistress the female, æsthetically, pretends to be. In this world of æsthetic make-believe our homes are not respectable; they would scorn to be so, for to the romantic female mind, when it occupies itself with art, the improper is the artistic.

But this needs a more precise demonstration. We wonder at our modern passion for superfluous ornament. We shall understand it only if we discover its origin. The King's mistress liked everything about her to be ornamented, because it was a point of honour with her to advertise the King's devotion to her in the costliness of all her surroundings. He loved her so much that he had paid for all this ornamentation. She, like Cleopatra, was always proving the potency of her charms by melting pearls in vinegar. Like a prize ox, she was hung with the trophies of her physical pre-eminence. In all the art which we call Louis Quinze there is this advertisement of the labour spent upon it. It proclaims that a vast deal of trouble has been taken in the making of it, and we can see the artist utterly subdued to this trouble, utterly the slave of the mistress's exorbitant whims. This advertisement of labour spent, without the reality, has been the mark of all popular domestic art ever since.

The beautiful is the ornamented—namely, that which looks as if it had taken a great deal of trouble to make. The trouble now is taken by machinery, and so, with the cost, is minimized ; and what it produces is ugliness, an ugliness which could not be mistaken for beauty but for the notion that it does express a desirable state of being in those who possess it. And this desirable state is the state of the King's mistress, of a siren who can have whatever she desires because of the potency of her charms. How otherwise can we explain the passion for superfluous machine-made ornament which makes our respectable homes so hideous ? The machine simulates a trouble that has not been taken, and so gives proof of a voluptuous infatuation that does not exist. The hardworking mother of a family buys out of her scanty allowance a scent-bottle that looks as if it had been laboriously cut for a King's mistress, whereas really it has been moulded by machinery to keep up the delusion, unconsciously cherished by her, that she lives in a world of irresistible and unscrupulous feminine charm. And her husband endures indulgently all this super-fluous ugliness because he, too, believes that it is the function of art to make the drawing-room of the mother of a family look like the boudoir of a siren.

Most of this make-believe remains uncon-scious. We are all so used to it that we do not see in it the expression of the dying harem instinct in women. Yet it persists, even where the harem instinct would be passionately repudiated. It persists often in the dress of the most defiant suffragette, in outbreaks of incongruous frivolity, forlorn tawdry roses that still whisper memories of the Pompadour and her triumphant guilty splendour.

But besides all this unconscious feminine influence upon art, there is the influence of women who care consciously for art; and it also has an enervating effect on the artist. For the female patron of art, just because there are so few male patrons of it, is apt to take a motherly interest in the artist. To her he is a delightful wayward child rather than a real man occupied with real things, like her husband or her father or her brother: not one who can earn money for her and fight for her and protect her, but rather one who needs to be protected and humoured in a world which cares so little for art. To her, with all her passion for art, it is something in its nature irrational, and, like a child, delightful because irrational. It is an escape from reality rather than a part of it. And so she will believe whatever the artist tells her because he is an artist, not because he is a man of sense; and she encourages him to be more of an artist than a man of sense. She encourages him to be extravagantly æsthetic, and enjoys all his extravagance as a diversion from the sound masculinity of her own mankind. There is room in her prosperous, easy world for these diversions from business, just as there is room for charity or, perhaps, religion. The world can afford artists as it can afford pets; as it can afford beautiful, cultivated women. And that also is the view of her husband, if he is good-natured. But to him, just because art and artists are the proper concern of his wife, they are even less serious than they are to her. She may persuade herself that she takes them quite seriously, but he pretends to do so only out of politeness, and as he would pretend to take her clothes seriously. For him the type of the artist is still the pianist who gives locks of his over-abundant hair to ladies. Even if the artist is a painter and cuts his hair and dresses like a man, he still belongs to the feminine world and excites himself about matters that do not concern men. Men can afford him, and so they tolerate him; but he is one of the expenses they would cut down if it were necessary to cut down expenses.

Well, it is necessary to cut down expenses now; and yet in ages much sterner and poorer than our own art was the concern of men, and they afforded it because it was not to them a mere feminine luxury. They afforded the towering churches of the Middle Ages because they expressed the religious passion of all mankind; and have we nothing to express except a dying harem instinct and the motherliness of kind women to a neglected class? We ought to be grateful to this motherliness, which has kept art alive in an age of ignorance; but we should see that it is only a *pis-aller*, and women should see this as well as men. The female attitude towards art has been itself the result of a wrong relation between women and men, a relation half-animal, half-romantic, and therefore not quite real. This relation, even while it has ceased to exist more and

The Pompadour in Art

more in fact, has still continued to express itself æsthetically; and in art it has become a mere obsolete nuisance. One may care nothing for art and yet long to be rid of the meaningless frivolities of our domestic art. One may wish to clear them away as so much litter and trash; and this clearance is necessary so that we may purge our vision and see what is beautiful. We are almost rid of the manners of the King's mistress, and most women no longer try to appeal to men by their charming unreason. It is not merely that the appeal fails now; they themselves refuse to make it, out of self-respect. But they still remain irrational in their tastes; or at least they have not learned that all this æsthetic irrationality misrepresents them, that it is forced upon them by tradesmen, that it is as inexpressive as a sentimental music-hall song sung by a gramophone. But now that men have given women the vote, and so proved that they take them seriously at last, they have the right to speak plainly on this matter. The feminine influence upon art has been bad. Let us admit that it has been the result of a bad masculine influence upon women, that it has been supreme because men have become philistine; but the fact remains that it has been bad. Art must be taken seriously if it is to be worth anything. It must be the expression of what is serious and real in the human mind. But all this feminine art has expressed, and has tried to glorify, something false and worthless. Therefore it has been ugly, and we are all sick of its ugliness. We look to women, now that they are equalled with men by an act of legal justice, to deliver us from it They disown the Pompadour in fact; let them disown her in art.

An Unpopular Master ◦ ◦ ◦

NICHOLAS POUSSIN is one of the great painters of the world; yet it is easier to give reasons for disliking him than for liking him. After his death there was a war of pamphlets about him; the one side, led by Lebrun, holding him up as a model for all painters to come, the other side, under de Piles, calling him a mere pedant compared with Rubens. Here is a passage from a poem against Poussin :—

> Il sçavoit manier la régle et le compas,
> Parloit de la lumière et ne l'entendoit pas ;
> Il estoit de l'antique un assez bon copiste,
> Mais sans invention, et mauvais coloriste.
> Il ne pouvait marcher que sur le pas d'autruy :
> Le génie a manqué, c'est un malheur pour luy.

Now this is just what the criticism of yesterday said about him, the criticism of the eighties and nineties, when it was supposed that Velasquez had discovered the art of seeing, and with

37

it the art of painting. It sounds plausible, but not a word of it is true. And yet it remains difficult to show why it is not true, to distinguish between the genius of Poussin and the pedantry of his imitators, to convince people that he was not a bad colourist, and that he did not imitate the antique.

This difficulty is connected with the age in which he happened to live. Nobody calls Mantegna a pedant nowadays; yet one might say against him most of the things that have been said against Poussin. But Mantegna lived in a century that we like, and Poussin in one that we dislike. The seventeenth century is for us a time of pictorial platitude; there was nothing then to discover about gesture or expression, and painters, even the best of them, used stock gestures and stock expressions without any of the eagerness of discovery. Now Poussin is, or appears to be, in many of his works a dramatic painter, and for us his drama is platitudinous. Take the "Plague of Ashdod," in the National Gallery. There are the gestures that we are already a little weary of in Raphael's cartoons. The figures express horror and fear with uplifted hands or contorted features; but their real business seems to be to make the picture. The drama

An Unpopular Master

is thrust upon us, and we cannot ignore it; yet
we feel that it is no discovery for the artist,
but something that he has learnt like a second-
rate actor—that he has, in fact, a "bag of
tricks" in common with all the Italian painters
of his time, and that he is only pretending to
be surprised by his subject. Now every age
has its artistic platitudes; but these platitudes of dramatic expression are peculiarly
wearisome to us because they have persisted in
European painting up to the present day, and
because most great painters in modern times
have struggled in one way or another to escape
from them. We associate them with medio-
crity and insincerity; and we do not understand that for many of the better painters of
the seventeenth century they were only a basis
for discoveries of a different kind. Il Greco,
for instance, is often as dramatically platitudinous as Guido Reni, but he also was making
discoveries in design which happen to interest
us now, so that we overlook his platitudes.
He was trying to express his emotions not so
much by gesture and the play of features as by
a rhythm really independent of those, a rhythm
carried through everything in the picture, to
which all his platitudes are subject. And
because this rhythm is new to us now we

39

hardly notice the platitudes. Poussin was playing the same game, but his rhythm has been imitated by so many dull painters that we are tempted to think it as platitudinous as his drama, and that is where we are unjust to him.

Poussin had a mind that was at once passionate and determined to be master of its passions. He would not suppress them, but he would express them with complete composure; and as Donne in poetry tried to attain to an intellectual mastery over his passions by means of conceits, so Poussin in painting tried to attain to the same mastery through the representation of an ideal world. Each was enthralled with his experience of real life; but each was dissatisfied with the haphazard, tyrannous nature of that experience, and especially with the divorce between passion and intellect, which in actual experience is so painful to the man who is both passionate and intelligent. So each, in his art, tried to make a new kind of experience, in which passion should be intelligent and intellect passionate. This, no doubt, is what every artist tries to do; but the effort was peculiarly fierce in Donne and Poussin because in them there was a more than common discord between passion and intelligence,

because they were instantly critical both of
what they desired and of their own process of
desire. Donne, at the very height of passion,
asked himself why he was passionate; and he
could not express his passion without trying to
justify it to his intelligence. So in his poetry
he endeavoured to experience it again with
simultaneous intellectual justification which in
that poetry was a part of the experience itself.
Poussin aims not so much at an intellectual
justification of passion as at an expression of it
in which there shall be also complete intellectual composure. He aims in his art at an
experience in which the intellect shall be free
from the bewilderment of the passions and the
passions also free from the check of the
intellect; and to this he attains by the representation of an ideal state in which the intellect can make all the forms through which the
passion expresses itself. He is, in fact, nearer
than most painters to the musician; but still
he is a painter and appeals to us through the
representation of objects that we can recognize
by their likeness to what we have seen ourselves. His intellect desires to make its forms,
not to have them imposed upon it by mere
ocular experience, since ocular experience for
him is full of the tyrannous bewilderment of

actual passion. But at the same time those forms which his intellect makes must be recognized by their likeness to what men see in the world about them. So he found a link between his ideal forms and what men see in what is vaguely called the antique.

But he did not go to the antique out of any artistic snobbery or because he distrusted his own natural taste. The antique was not for him an aristocratic world of art that he tried to enter in the hope of becoming himself an aristocrat. He showed that he was perfectly at ease in that world by the manner in which he painted its subjects. When, for instance, he paints Bacchanals, he is really much less overawed by the subject than Rubens would be. Rubens, who was a man of culture and an intellectual *parvenu*, tried desperately to combine his natural tastes with classical subjects. When he painted a Flemish cook as Venus he really tried to make her look like Venus; and the result is a Flemish cook pretending to be Venus, an incongruity that betrays a like incongruity in the artist's mind. Poussin's Venus, far less flesh and blood, does belong entirely to the world in which he imagines her—indeed, so intensely that, if we have lost interest in that world, she fails to interest us. The Vene-

tians have done this much better, we think;
and why, if Poussin was going to paint like
Titian, did he not use Titian's colour? The
answer is, Because his mood was very far from
Titian's, because he makes a comment that
Titian never makes upon his Venuses and
Bacchanals. Rubens makes no comment at all :
his attitude towards the classical is that of
the wondering *parvenu*. Titian through the
classical expresses the Renaissance liberation
from scruple and fear. But Poussin gives us a
mortal comment upon this immortal careless-
ness and delight. Whether his figures are
tranquil or rapturous, there is in his colour an
expression of something far from their felicity.
Indeed, however voluptuous the forms may be,
the colour is always ascetic. It is not that he
seems to disapprove of those glorified pleasures
of the senses, but that he cannot satisfy himself with his own conception of them, as Titian
could. Titian represents a world in which all
the mind consents to delight. His figures
are not foolish, but they are like dancers or
dreamers to the music of their own pleasure.
He makes us hear that music to which his
figures dance or dream; but, with Poussin, we
do not hear it, we only see the figures subject
to it as to some influence from which we

are cut off; and that which cuts us off is the colour.

Most painters, if they wished to paint a scene of voluptuous pleasure, would conceive it first in colour; for colour is the natural expression of all delights of the senses. But Poussin never allows the delight that he paints to affect his colour at all. That is always an expression of his own permanent mind, of a mind that could not dance or dream to the music of any pleasure possible in this world. For him the ideal world was not merely one of perpetual, intensified pleasure, but one in which all the activities of the mind should work like gratified senses and yet keep their own character, in which passion should be freed from its bewilderment and intellect from its questioning. That was what he tried to represent; and his colour was a comment, half-unconscious perhaps, upon its impossibility. For the everlasting conflict between colour and form does itself express that impossibility. Whatever he might represent, Poussin could not, for one moment, lose his interest in form or subordinate it to colour. His figures, whatever their raptures, must express his own intellectual mastery of them; and it was impossible to combine this with a

An Unpopular Master

colour that should express their raptures. But Poussin, knowing this impossibility, was not content with a compromise. He might have used a faintly agreeable colour that would not be incongruous with their raptures; but he chose rather to express his own exasperation in a colour that was violently incongruous with them, but which at the same time heightens his emphasis upon form. So, though there is an incongruity between the subject itself and the mood in which it is treated, there is none in the treatment. Poussin himself seems to look, and to make us look, at a mythological Paradise, with the searching, mournful gaze of a human spectator. This glory is forbidden to us not merely by our circumstances but by the nature of our own minds. It is, indeed, one of our own conceptions of Heaven, but inadequate like all the rest; and Poussin, by making the conception clear to us, reveals its inadequacy.

He paints the subjects of the Renaissance like a man remembering his own youth, and sad, not because he has lost the pleasures of youth, but because he wasted himself upon them. Here are these deities, he seems to tell us, but there must be a secret in their felicity that we do not understand. The joy they seem to offer is below us, and he will not pre-

45

tend to have caught it from them in his art.
For that art is always sad, not with a particular grief nor with mere low spirits, but with
the incongruity of the passions and the intellect; and this noble sadness is expressed by
Poussin as no other painter has expressed it.
He was himself a melancholy man to whom art
was the one happiness of life; but he did not
use his art to talk of his sorrows. He used it
to create a world of clear and orderly design,
and satisfied his intellect in the creation of it.
In his art he could exercise the composure
which actual experience disturbed; he could
remake that reality so troubled by the conflict
of sense, emotion, and understanding; but,
even in remaking it, he added the comment
that it was only his in art. And that is the
reason why his art seems so impersonal to us,
why there is the same cold passion in all his
pictures, whether religious or mythological.
In all of them he expresses a sharp dissatisfaction with the very nature of his actual experience. A painter like Rubens is entranced
with his own actual vision of things; but
Poussin tells us that he has never even seen
anything as he wanted to see it. He is
not a vague idealist dissatisfied with reality
because of the weakness of his own senses or

An Unpopular Master

understanding. Rather he seems to cry, like Poe, of everything that he draws—

> O God, can I not grasp
> Them with a tighter clasp?

It is the very substance and matter of things that he tries to master; and that so intensely that he never sees them flushed or dimmed by any mood of his own. Nor does he allow the passions of his figures to affect his representation of them or of their surroundings. He is cold, himself, towards these passions, for to him they are only a part of the bewilderment of actual experience. But in making forms he escapes from that bewilderment and shows us matter utterly subject to mind. Yet in this triumph there is always implied the sadness that such a triumph is impossible in life, that the artist cannot be what he paints. The Renaissance had failed, and Poussin's art was a bitterly sincere announcement of its failure.

A Defence of Criticism ✑ ✑ ✑

THE only kind of critic taken seriously in
England is the art critic; and he is
taken seriously as an expert, that is to say, as
one who will tell us not what he has found in
a work of art, but who produced it. His very
judgment is valued not on a matter of art at
all, but on a matter of business. No one
wants to know whether a certain picture is
good or bad. The question is, Was it painted
by Romney? It might well have been and
yet be a very bad picture; but that is not the
point. Experts are called to say that it is by
Romney; and they are proved to be wrong.
Thereupon Sir Thomas Jackson writes to the
Times and says that if people learned to think
for themselves the profession of art critic
would be at an end. The art critic, for him,
is one who tells people what to think. And
then he proceeds—

It is only for the public he writes; he is of
no use to artists. I doubt whether any man in
any branch of art could be found who would

honestly say he had ever learned anything from the art critic, who, after all, is only an amateur. The criticism we value, and that which really helps, is that of our brother artists, often sharp and unsparing, but always salutary and useful. And if useless to the artist, art criticism is harmful to the public, who take their opinion from it at second hand. Were all art criticism made penal for ten years lovers of art would learn to think for themselves, and a truer appreciation of art than the commercial one would result, with the greatest benefit both to art and to artists. It is the artist and not the professional critic who should be the real instructor of the public taste.

Here there seems to be an inconsistency; for if we are to think for ourselves we do not need to be instructed by artists any more than by critics. But Sir Thomas Jackson may mean that the artist is to instruct the public only through his works. Still, the question remains, How is the artist to be recognized? There is a riddle—When is an artist not an artist? and the answer is—Nine times out of ten. Certainly the opinions of artists about each other will not bring security to the public mind; and does Sir T. Jackson really believe that artists always value the criticism of brother artists? Does an Academician value the criticism of a Vorticist, or *vice versa?* The Academician, of course, would say that the Vorticist was not an artist—and *vice versa.* The artist values the opinion of the artist who agrees with him ; and at present there is less agreement among artists than among critics. They condemn each other more than the critics condemn them.

But these are minor points. What I am concerned with is Sir T. Jackson's notion of the function of criticism. For him, as for most Englishmen, the critic is one who tells people what to think ; and the value of his criticism depends upon his reputation ; we should pay no heed to art critics, because they are not artists. But the critic, whether of art or of anything else, is a writer; and he is to be judged not by his reputation either as artist or as critic, but by what he writes. Sir T. Jackson thinks that he is condemning the critic when he says that he writes only for the public. He might as well think that he condemned the artist if he said that he worked only for the public. Of course the critic writes for the public, as the painter paints for the public ; and he writes as one of the public, not as an artist. Further, if he is a critic, he does not write to tell the public what to think

A Defence of Criticism

any more than he writes to tell the painter how to paint. Just as the painter in his pictures expresses a general interest in the visible world, so the critic in his criticism expresses a general interest in art; and his justification, like that of the painter, consists in his power of expressing this interest. If he cannot express it well, it is useless to talk about his reputation either as artist or critic; one might as well excuse a bad picture of a garden by saying that the painter of it was a good gardener and therefore a good judge of gardens.

It is a misfortune that the word critic should be derived from a Greek word meaning judge. A critic certainly does arrive at judgments; but the value of his criticism, if it has any, consists not in the judgment, but in the process by which it is arrived at. This fact is seldom understood in England, either by the public or by artists. The artist cares only about the judgment and complains that a mere amateur has no right to judge him. He would rather be judged by himself; and, being himself an artist, he must be a better judge. But the question to be asked about the critic is not whether he is an amateur as an artist, but whether he is an amateur as a critic;

and that can be decided only by his criticism.
The greatest artist might prove that he was
an amateur in criticism; and he could not dis-
prove it by appealing to his art. Sir Joshua
Reynolds, for instance, thinks like an amateur
in some of his discourses; and it is amateur
thinking to defend him by saying that he does
not paint like one.

Certainly much of our criticism consists of
mere judgments, and is therefore worthless as
criticism. But much of our art consists also
of mere judgments; it tells us nothing except
that the artist admires this or that, or believes
that the public admires it; and it also is
worthless as art. But no critic therefore
writes to the papers to say that, if only the
public would learn to feel for themselves, the
profession of artist would be at an end. We
know that the business of an artist is not to
tell the public what to feel about the visible
world, or anything else, but to express his
own interest in the visible world or whatever
may be the subject-matter of his art. We
do not condemn art because of its failures.
Those who know anything at all about the
nature of art know that it has value because it
expresses the common interests of mankind
better than most men can express them; and

A Defence of Criticism

for this reason it has value for mankind and
not merely for artists. For this reason, also,
criticism has value for mankind and not merely
for artists or for critics. But the value of it
does not lie in the judgment of the critic any
more than the value of art lies in the judgment, taste, preference of the artist. The
value in both cases lies in power of expression;
and by that art and criticism are to be
judged.

Needless to say, then, criticism is not to be
judged by the help it gives to artists. One
might as well suppose that philosophy was to
be judged by the help it gives to the Deity.
The philosopher does not tell the Deity how
He ought to have made the universe; nor do
we read philosophy for the sake of the judgments at which philosophers arrive. We do
not want to know Kant's opinion because he
is Kant; what interests us is the process by
which he arrives at that opinion, and it is the
process which convinces us that his opinion is
right, if we are convinced. So it is, or should
be, with criticism. It ought to provoke thought
rather than to suppress it; and if it does not
provoke thought it is worthless.

But in the best criticism judgment is rather
implied than expressed. For the proper

53

subject-matter of criticism is the experience of
works of art. The best critic is he who has
experienced a work of art so intensely that his
criticism is the spontaneous expression of his
experience. He tells us what has happened to
him, as the artist tells us what has happened
to him; and we, as we read, do not judge
either the criticism or the art criticized, but
share the experience. The value of art lies in
the fact that it communicates the experience
and the experiencing power of one man to
many. When we hear a symphony of
Beethoven, we are for the moment Beethoven;
and we ourselves are enriched for ever by the
fact that we have for the moment been
Beethoven. So the value of the best criticism
lies in the fact that it communicates the experience and the experiencing power of the
critic to his readers and so enriches their
experiencing power. If he is futile, so is the
artist. If we cannot read him without danger
to our own independence of thought, neither
can we look at a picture without danger to our
own independence of vision. But believe in
the fellowship of mankind, believe that one
mind can pour into another and enrich it with
its own treasures, and you will know that
neither art nor criticism is futile. They stand

A Defence of Criticism

or fall together, and the artist who condemns the critic condemns himself also.

There remains the contention, half implied by Sir T. Jackson, that the critic's experience of art is of no value because he is not an artist. Now if it is of no value to himself because he is not an artist, then art is of no value to anyone except the artist, and the artist who practises the same kind of art; music is of value only to musicians, and painting to painters. It cannot be that mere technical training gives a man the mysterious power of experiencing works of art; for, as we all know, it does not make an artist. No artist will admit that anyone through technical training can become a member of the sacred brotherhood of those who understand the mystery of art. Therefore they had all better admit that there is no mystery about it, or, rather, a mystery for us all. Either art is of value to us all, and our own experience of it is of value to us; or art has no value whatever to anyone, but is the meaningless activity of a few oddities who would be better employed in agriculture.

But if our own experience of art is of value to us, then it is possible for us to communicate that experience to others so that it may be of value to them; as it is possible for the painter to communicate to others his experience of the visible world. If he denies this, once again he denies himself. He shuts himself within the prison of his own arrogance, from which he can escape only by a want of logic. But, further, if our experience of art is of value to ourselves, and if it is possible for us to communicate that experience to others, it is also possible for us to arrive at conclusions about that experience which may be of value both to ourselves and to others. Hence scientific or philosophic criticism, which is based not, as some artists seem to think, upon a fraudulent pretence of the critic that he himself is an artist, but upon that experience of art which is, or may be, common to all men. The philosophic critic writes not as one who knows how to produce that which he criticizes better than he who has produced it, but as one who has experienced art; and his own experience is really the subject-matter of his criticism. If he *is* a philosophic critic, he will know that his experience is itself necessarily imperfect. As some one has said: " We do not judge works of art; they judge us "; and the critic is to be judged by the manner in which he has experienced art, as the painter is to be judged by the manner in which he has experienced the visible

A Defence of Criticism

world. All the imperfections of his experience will be betrayed in his criticism; where he is insensitive, there he will fail, both as artist and as philosopher; and of this fact he must be constantly aware. So if he gives himself the airs of a judge, if he relies on his own reputation to make or mar the reputation of a work of art, he ceases to be a critic and deserves all that artists in their haste have said about him. Still, it is a pity that artists, in their haste, should say these things; for when they do so they, too, become critics of the wrong sort, critics insensitive to criticism. They may think that they are upholding the cause of art; but they are upholding the cause of stupidity, that common enemy of art and of criticism.

The Artist and his Audience ○ ○

ACCORDING to Whistler art is not a social activity at all; according to Tolstoy it is nothing else. But art is clearly a social activity and something more; yet no one has yet reconciled the truth in Whistler's doctrine with the truth in Tolstoy's. Each leaves out an essential part of the truth, and they remain opposed in their mixture of error and truth. The main point of Whistler's "Ten o'clock" is that art is not a social activity. "Listen," he cries, "there never was an artistic period. There never was an art-loving nation. In the beginning man went forth each day—some to battle, some to the chase; others again to dig and to delve in the field—all that they might gain and live or lose and die. Until there was found among them one, differing from the rest, whose pursuits attracted him not, and so he stayed by the tents with the women, and traced strange devices with a burnt stick upon a gourd. This man, who took no joy in the ways of his

The Artist and his Audience

brethren, who cared not for conquest and fretted in the field, this designer of quaint patterns, this deviser of the beautiful, who perceived in Nature about him curious curvings, as faces are seen in the fire—this dreamer apart was the first artist."

Then, he says, the hunters and the workers drank from the artists' goblets, "taking no note the while of the craftsman's pride, and understanding not his glory in his work; drinking at the cup not from choice, not from a consciousness that it was beautiful, but because, forsooth, there was none other!" Luxury grew, and the great ages of art came. "Greece was in its splendour, and art reigned supreme —by force of fact, not by election. And the people questioned not, and had nothing to say in the matter." In fact art flourished because mankind did not notice it. But "there arose a new class, who discovered the cheap, and foresaw fortune in the manufacture of the sham." Then, according to Whistler, a strange thing happened. "The heroes filled from the jugs and drank from the bowls — with understanding. . . . And the people — this time — had much to say in the matter, and all were satisfied. And Birmingham and Manchester arose in their

59

might, and art was relegated to the curiosity shop."

Whistler does not explain why, if no one was aware of the existence of art except the artist, those who were not artists began to imitate it. If no one prized art, why should sham art have come into existence? According to him it was the sham that made men aware of the true; yet the sham could not exist until men were aware of the true. But the account he gives of the decadence of art is historically untrue as well as unintelligible. We know little of the primitive artist; but we have no proof that he was utterly different from other men, or that they did not enjoy his activities. If they had not enjoyed them they would probably have killed him. The primitive artist survived, no doubt, because he was an artist in his leisure; and all we know of more primitive art goes to prove that it was, and is, practised not by a special class but by the ordinary primitive man in his leisure. Peasant art is produced by peasants, not by lonely artists. Some, of course, have more gift for it than others, but all enjoy it, though they do not call it art. Whistler saw himself in every primitive artist; and seeing himself as a dreamer apart misunderstood by the common herd, he saw the primi-

tive artist as one living in a primitive White
House, and producing primitive nocturnes for
his own amusement, unnoticed, happily, by
primitive critics.

But his view, though refuted both by history
and by common sense, is still held by many
artists and amateurs. They themselves make
much of art, but do not see that their theory
makes little of it, makes it a mere caprice of
the human mind, like the collecting of postage
stamps. If art has any value or importance
for mankind, it is because it is a social activity.
If no one but an artist can enjoy art, it seems
to follow that no art can be completely enjoyed
except by him who has produced it; for in
relation to that art he alone is an artist. All
other artists, even, are the public; and, according to Whistler, the public has nothing to do
with art; it flourishes best when they are not
aware of its existence. He is very contemptu-
ous of taste. All judgment of art must be
based on expert knowledge, for art, he says,
"is based upon laws as rigid and defined as
those of the known sciences." Yet whereas
"no polished member of society is at all
affected by admitting himself neither engineer,
mathematician, nor astronomer, and therefore
remains willingly discreet and taciturn upon

these subjects, still he would be highly offended were he supposed to have no voice in what clearly to him is a matter of taste." So to Whistler art has no more to do with the life of the ordinary man than astronomy or mathematics. His mention of engineering is an unfortunate slip, for, although we are not engineers we all knew, when the Tay Bridge broke down and threw hundreds of passengers into the water, that it was not a good bridge. We are all concerned with engineering in spite of our ignorance of it, because we make use of its works. Whistler assumes that we make no use of works of art except as objects of use; and since pictures, poems, music are not objects of use, we can have no concern with them whatever—which is absurd.

But here comes Tolstoy, who tells us that all works of art are merely objects of use and are to be judged therefore by the extent of their use. A work of art that few can enjoy fails as much as a railway that few can travel by. "Art," Tolstoy says, "is a human activity, consisting in this—that one man consciously, by means of certain external signs, hands on to others feelings he has lived through, and that other people are infected by these feelings and also experience them." So it is the essence of

The Artist and his Audience

a work of art that it shall infect others with
the feelings of the artist. Now certainly a
work of art is a work of art to us only if it
does so infect us, but Tolstoy is not content
with that. The individual is not to judge the
work of art by its infection of himself. He is
to consider also the extent of its infection.
"For a work to be esteemed good and to be
approved of and diffused it will have to satisfy
the demands, not of a few people living in
identical and often unnatural conditions, but
it will have to satisfy the demands of all those
great masses of people who are situated in the
natural conditions of laborious life."

The two views are utterly irreconcilable.
According to Whistler the public are not to
judge art at all because they have no concern
with it, and it flourishes most when they do
not pretend to have any concern with it.
According to Tolstoy the individual is to
judge it, not by the effect it produces on him,
but by the effect it produces on others, "on all
those great masses of people who are situated
in the natural conditions of laborious life."

Now, if we find ourselves intimidated by one
or other of these views, if we seem forced to
accept one of them against our will, it is a relief
and liberation from the tyranny of Whistler's

or Tolstoy's logic to ask ourselves simply what does actually happen to us in our own experience and enjoyment of a work of art. The fact that we are able to enjoy and experience a work of art does liberate us at once from the tyranny of Whistler; for clearly, if we can experience and enjoy a work of art, we are concerned with it. It is vain for Whistler to tell us that we ought not to be, or that we do injury to art by our concern. The fact of our enjoyment and experience makes art for us a social activity; we know that our enjoyment of it is good; we know also that the artist likes us to enjoy it; and we do not believe that either the primitive artist or the primitive man was different from us in this respect. There is now, and always has been, some kind of social relation between the artist and the public; the only question is how far that relation is the essence of art.

Tolstoy tells us that it is the essence of art, because the proper aim of art is to do good. This is implied in his doctrine that art can be good only if it is intelligible to most men. "The assertion that art may be good art and at the same time incomprehensible to a great number of people, is extremely unjust; and its consequences are ruinous to art itself." The

word unjust implies the moral factor. I am
not to enjoy a work of art if I know that
others cannot enjoy it, because it is not fair
that I should have a pleasure not shared by
them. If I know that others cannot share it,
I am to take no account of my own experience,
but to condemn the work, however good it
may seem to me. From this logic also I can
liberate myself by concerning myself simply
with my own experience. Again, if I experience and enjoy a work of art, I know that my
experience of it is good; and, in my judgment
of the work of art, I do not need to ask myself
how many others enjoy it. I may wish them
to enjoy it and try to make them do so, but
that effort of mine is not æsthetic but moral.
It does not affect my judgment of the work of
art, but is a result of that judgment. And, as
a matter of fact, if I am to experience a work
of art at all, I cannot be asking myself how
many others enjoy it. Judgments of art are
not formed in that way and cannot be; they
are, and must be, always formed out of our
own experience of art. If art is to be art to
us, we cannot think of it in terms of something
else. There would be no public for art at all
if we all agreed to judge it in terms of each
other's enjoyment or understanding. Each

individual of " the great masses of people who are situated in the natural conditions of laborious life " would also have to ask himself whether the rest of the masses were enjoying and understanding, before he could judge; indeed, he would not feel a right to enjoy until he knew that the rest were enjoying. That is to say, no individual would ever enjoy art at all. The fact is that art is produced by the individual artist and experienced by the individual man. Tolstoy says that it is experienced by mankind in the mass, and not as individuals; Whistler that it is not experienced at all, either by the mass or by the individual. Each is a heretic with some truth in his heresy; what is the true doctrine?

It is clear that every artist desires an audience, not merely so that he may win pudding and praise from them, nor so that he may do them good; none of these aims will make him an artist; he can accomplish all of them without attempting to produce a work of art. It is also clear that his artistic success is not his success in winning an audience. Those " great masses of people who are situated in the natural conditions of laborious life " are a figment of Tolstoy's mind. No conditions are natural in the sense in which he uses the word;

nor do any existing conditions make one man a better judge of art than another. There is no multitude of simple, normal, unspoilt men able and willing to enjoy any real art that is presented to them. The right experience of art comes with effort, like right thought and right action; and no Russian peasant has it because he works in the fields. Nor, on the other hand, are there any artists who are mere "sports" occupied with a queer game of their own self-expression which no one else can enjoy. There is a necessary relation between the work of art and its audience, even if no actual audience for it exists; and the fact that this relation must be, even when there is no audience in existence, is the paradox and problem of art. A work of art claims an audience, entreats it, is indeed made for it; but must have it on its own terms. Men are artists because they are men, because they have a faculty, at its height, which is shared by all men. In that Croce is right; and his doctrine that all men are artists in some degree, and that the very experience of art is itself an æsthetic activity, contains a truth of great value. But his æsthetic ignores, or seems to ignore, the fact that art is not merely, as he calls it, expression, but is also a means of address; in fact, that we do not express ourselves except when we address ourselves to others, even though we speak to no particular, or even existing, audience. Yet this fact is obvious; for all art gets its very form from the fact that it is a method of address. A story is a story because it is told, and told to some one not the teller. A picture is a picture because it is painted to be seen. It has all its artistic qualities because it is addressed to the eye. And music is music, and has the form which makes it music, because it is addressed to the ear. Without this intention of address there could be no form in art and no distinction between art and day-dreaming. Day-dreaming is not expression, is not art, because it is addressed to no one but is a purposeless activity of the mind. It becomes art only when there is the purpose of address in it. That purpose will give it form and turn it from day-dreaming into art. Even in an object of use which is also a work of art, the art is the effort of the maker to emphasize, that is, to point out, the beauty of that which he has made. It is this emphasis that turns building into architecture; and it implies that the building is made not merely for the builder's or for anyone else's use, but that its aim also is to address an audience, to

The Artist and his Audience

speak to the eye as a picture speaks to it. Art is made for men as surely as boots are made for them.

But not as Tolstoy thinks, for any particular class of men or even for the whole mass of existing mankind. The artist will not and cannot judge his work by its effects on any actual men, any more than we can or will judge it by its effects on anyone except ourselves. As we, in our experience of it, must be completely individual; so must he in his production of it. He is not a public servant, but a man speaking for himself, and with no thought of effects, to anyone who will hear. His audience consists only of those who will hear, of those individuals who can understand his individual expression which is also communication. In his art he seeks the individual who will hear. He has something to say; but he can say it only to others, not to himself; it is what it is because he says it to others. Yet he says it also for its own sake and not for theirs. The particular likes and dislikes, stupidities, limitations, demands, of individual men or classes are nothing to him. The condition of his art is this alone, that he does address it to an audience. So the relation between the artist and his audience is the most important fact of his art, even if he has no actual audience. It is his attitude towards the audience that makes him do his best or his worst, makes him a good artist or a bad one, that sets him free to express all he has to say or hampers him with inhibitions. His business is not to find an audience, but to find the right attitude towards one, the attitude which is that of the artist and not of the tradesman, or peacock, or philanthropist. And it is plain that in his effort to find this right attitude he may be helped or hindered much by his actual fellow-men. The artist is also a man and subject to all the temptations of men. Whistler, when he said that art happens, ignored this fact, ignored the whole social relation of mankind and the whole history of the arts; while Tolstoy ignored no less the mind of the artist, and the minds of all those who do actually experience art. To Whistler the artist is a *Chimæra bombinans in vacuo*; to Tolstoy he is a philanthropist. For Whistler the public has no function whatever in relation to art; for Tolstoy the artist himself has no function whatever except a moral one. In fact he denies the existence of the artist, as Whistler denies the existence of the public. Whistler's truth is that the public must not tell the artist

The Artist and his Audience

what he is to do; Tolstoy's, that a public with a right relation to the artist will help the artist to have a right relation to the public.

Artists are not "sports," but men; and men engaged in one of the most difficult of human activities. They are subject to æsthetic temptation and sin, as all men are subject to temptation and sin of all kinds. Their public may tempt them to think more of themselves than of what they have to express, either by perverse admiration or by ignorant contempt. An actual audience may be an obstruction between them and the ideal audience to which every artist should address himself. Every artist must desire that his ideal audience should exist, and may mistake an actual audience for it. In the ideal relation between an artist and his audience, it is the universal in him that speaks to the universal in them, and yet this universal finds an intensely personal expression. Art, which is personal expression, tells, not of what the artist wants, but of what he values. But if his ego is provoked by the ego in a particular audience, then he begins to tell of what he wants or of what they want. The audience may demand of him that he shall please them by indulging their particular vanities, appetites, sentimental desires, that he

shall present life to them as they wish it to be ;
and if he yields to that demand it is because of
the demands of his own particular ego.   There
is a transaction between him and that audience,
in its essence commercial.   His art is the
particular supplying some kind of goods to the
particular, not the universal pouring itself out
to the universal.

The function of the audience is not to
demand but to receive.   It should not allow
its own expectations to hinder its receptiveness ;
to that extent Whistler is right.   Art happens
as the beauty of the universe happens ; and it
is the business of the audience to experience it,
not to dictate how it shall happen.   It has
been said : It is not we who judge works of
art ; they judge us.   The artist speaks and we
listen ; but still he speaks to us and by listen-
ing wisely we help him to speak his best, for
man is a social being ; and all life, in so far as
it is what it wishes to be, is a fellowship.
Never is it so completely a fellowship as in the
relation between an artist and his audience.
There Tolstoy is right, but the fellowship has
to be achieved by both the artist and the
audience.   There is no body of simple peasants,
any more than there are rich or cultured
people, to whom he must address himself or

The Artist and his Audience

whose demands he must satisfy. Art that tries to satisfy any particular demand is of use neither to the flesh nor to the spirit. It is neither meat nor music. But where all is well with it, the spirit in the artist speaks to the spirit in his audience. There is a common quality in both, with which he speaks and they listen; and where this common quality is found art thrives.

Wilfulness and Wisdom ✧ ✧ ✧

THERE are people to whom the war was merely the running amuck of a criminal lunatic; and they get what pleasure they can from calling that lunatic all the names they can think of. To them the Germans are different in kind from all other peoples, utterly separated from the rest of us by their crimes. We could learn nothing from them except how to crush them; and, having done so, we shall need to learn nothing except how to keep them down. But such minds never learn anything from experience, because they believe that there is nothing to be learnt. They consume all their mental energy in anger and the expression of it; and in doing so they grow more and more like those with whom they are angry. Wisdom always goes contrary to what our passions tell us, especially when they take the form of righteous indignation. The creative power of the mind begins with refusal of all those tempting fierce delights which the passions offer to it. Wisdom must be cold before it can

74

become warm; it must suppress the comforting
heat of the flesh before it can kindle with the
pure fire of the spirit. Above all, when we
say that we are not as other men, as the
Germans, for instance, it must insist that we
are, and that we shall avoid the German crime
only by recognizing our likeness to those who
have committed it.

The Germans have committed the great
crime; but they have been born and nurtured
in an atmosphere which made that crime possible; and we live in the same atmosphere.
Their error, though they carried it to an
extreme in theory and in practice with the
native extravagance of their race, is the error
of the whole Western world; and we shall not
understand what it is unless we are aware of it
in ourselves as well as in them. For it is a
world-error and one against which men have
been warned for ages; but in their pride they
will not listen to the warning. Many of the
old warnings, in the Gospels and elsewhere,
sound like platitudes to us; we expect the
clergyman to repeat them in church; but we
should never think of applying them to this
great, successful, progressive Western world of
ours. If we are not happy; if we do not even
see the way to happiness; if all our power

merely helps us to destroy each other, or to make the rich more vulgarly rich and the poor more squalidly poor; if the great energy of Germany has hurried her to her own ruin; still we do not ask whether we may not have made some fundamental mistake about our own nature and the nature of the universe, and whether Germany has not merely made it more systematically and more philosophically than the rest of us.

But the German, because he is systematic and philosophical, may reveal to us what that error is in us as well as in himself. We do not state it as if it were a splendid truth; we merely act upon it. He stated it for us with such histrionic and towering absurdity that we can laugh at his statement of it; but we must not laugh at him without learning to laugh at ourselves. All this talk about the iron will, about set teeth and ruthlessness, what does it mean except that the German chose to glorify openly and to carry to a logical extreme the peculiar error of the whole Western world— the belief that the highest function of man is to work his will upon people and things outside him, that he can change the world without changing himself?

The Christian doctrine, preached so long in

Wilfulness and Wisdom

vain and now almost forgotten, is the opposite
of this. It insists that man is by nature a
passive, an experiencing creature, and that he
can do nothing well in action unless he has
first learned a right passivity. Only by that
passivity can he enrich himself; and when he
has enriched himself he will act rightly. Man
has a will; but he must apply it at the right
point, or it will seem to him merely a blind
impulse. He must apply it to the manner in
which he experiences things; he must free himself from his " will to live " or his " will to
power," and see all men and things not as they
are of material use to him, but with the object
of loving whatever there is of beauty or virtue
in them. ' His will, in fact, must be the will to
love, which is the will to experience in a certain
way; and out of that will to love right action
will naturally ensue. Is this a platitude? If
it is, it is flatly contradicted by the German
doctrine of wilfulness. For the Germanic hero
exercises his will always upon other men and
things, not upon himself; and we all admire
this Germanic hero, when he is not an obvious
danger to us all, and when he is not made
ridiculous by the German presentment of him.
We all believe that the will is to be exercised
first of all in action, that it is the function of

the great man to change the world, not
to change himself. To us the great man is
one who does work a change upon the world,
no matter what that change may be. He may
change it only as an explosion changes things,
and at the end he may be left among the ruins
he has made; but still we admire him. We
compare him to the forces of nature, we say
that there is "something elemental" in him,
even though he has been merely an elemental
nuisance. We value force in itself, and do not
ask what it can find to value in itself when it
has exhausted itself upon the world. But out
of this worship of wilfulness there comes, sooner
or later, a profound scepticism and discourage-
ment. For while these wilful heroes do produce some violent effect, it is not the effect
they aimed at. Something happens; something has happened to Germany as the result
of Bismarck's wilfulness; but it is not what he
willed. The wilful hero is a cause in that he
acts; but the effect is not what he designed,
and so he seems to himself, and to the world,
only a link in an unending chain of cause and
effect; and as for his sense of will, it is nothing
but the illusion that he is all cause and not at
all effect.

Quem Deus vult perdere dementat prius.

Wilfulness and Wisdom

That old tag puts a truth wrongly. God does not interfere to afflict the wilful man with madness, but he has never thrown himself open to the wisdom of God. His mind is like a machine that acts with increasing speed and fury because there is less and less material for it to act upon. One act leads to another in a blind chain of cause and effect; he does this merely because he has done that, and seems to be driven by fate on and on to his own ruin. So it was with Napoleon in his later years. He had lost the sense of any reality whatever except his own action; he saw the world as a passive object to be acted upon by himself. And that is how the Germans saw it two years ago. They could not understand that it was possible for the world to react against them. It was merely something that they were going to remake, to work their will upon. The war, at its beginning, was not to them a conflict between human beings; it was a process by which they would make of things what they willed. There was no reality except in themselves and their own will; for, in their worship of action, they had lost the sense of external reality, they had come to believe that there was nothing to learn from it except what a craftsman learns from his material by working in it. It is by making that he learns; and they thought that there was no learning except by making.

But that is the mistake of the whole Western world, though we have none of us carried it so far as Germany. Other men are to us still men, they still have some reality to us; but we see external reality as a material for us to work in; we are to ourselves entirely active and not at all passive beings. Even among all the evil and sorrow of the war we still took a pride in the enormous power of our instruments of destruction, as if we were children playing with big, dangerous toys. But these toys are themselves the product of a society that must always be making and never thinking or feeling. They express the will for action that has ousted the will to experience; and all the changes which we work on the face of the earth express that will too. We could not live in the cities we have made for ourselves if we thought that we had anything to learn from the beauty of the earth. They are for us merely places in which we learn to act, in which no one could learn to think or feel. Passive experience is impossible in them and they do not consider the possibility of it. So they express in every building, in every

object, in the very clothes of their inhabit-
ants, an utter poverty of passive experience.
In what we make we give out no stored
riches of the mind; we make only so that we
may act, never so that we may express ourselves; and we have little art because our
making is entirely wilful. Our attempts at
art are themselves entirely wilful. We will
have art, we say; and so we plaster our utilities
with the ornaments of the past, as if we could
get the richness of experience secondhand from
our ancestors. And in the same way we are
always finding for our blind activities moral
motives, those motives which are real only
when they spring out of right experience. We
rationalize all that we do, but the rationalizing
is secondhand ornament to blind impulse; it
is an attempt to persuade ourselves that our
actions spring out of the experience which we
lack. There is among us an incessant activity
both of thought and of art; but much of it is
entirely wilful. The thinker makes theories to
justify what is done; he, too, sees all life in
terms of action, he is the parasite of action.
For a German professor the whole process of
history was but a prelude to the wilfulness of
Germany; he could not experience the past
except in terms of what Germany willed to do;

and the aim of his theorizing was to remove all scrupulous impediments to the action of Germany which she may have inherited from the past. Think so that you may be stronger to do what you wish to do; that is the modern notion of thought, and that is the reason why we throw up theories so easily; for thinking of this kind needs no experience, it needs merely an activity of the mind, the activity which collects facts and does with them what it will. And these theories are eagerly accepted so long as the impulse lasts which they justify. When that is spent they are forgotten, and new theories take their place to justify fresh impulses. And so it is with the incessant new movements in art. Art now is conceived entirely as action. The artist is as wilful as the Germanic hero; the will to make excludes in him the will to experience. The painter cannot look at the visible world without considering at once what kind of picture he will make of it. It is to him mere passive material for his artistic will, not an independent reality to enrich his mind so that it will give out its riches in the form of art. And as he is always willing to make pictures so he must will the kind of pictures he will make, as the Germans willed the kind of world they would make.

Wilfulness and Wisdom

But this willing of his is a kind of theorizing to justify his own action; and it changes incessantly because he never can be satisfied with his own poverty of experience. But still he will do anything rather than try to enrich that poverty.

And that is the secret of all our restlessness, the restlessness that forced the Germans into the folly and crime of war. We are always dissatisfied with our poverty of experience; and we try to get rid of our dissatisfaction in more blind activity, throwing up new theories all the while as reasons why we should act. We fidget about the earth as if we were children, that could not read, left in a library; and, like them, we do mischief. And that is just what we are: children that have not learnt to read let loose upon the library of the universe; and all that we can do is to pull the books about and play games with them and scribble on their pages. Everywhere the earth is defaced with our meaningless scribbling, and we tell ourselves that it means something because we want to scribble. Or sometimes we tell ourselves that there is no meaning in anything, no more in the books than in our scribble.

The only remedy is that we should learn to

read; and for this we need above all things humility; not merely the personal humility of a man who knows that other men excel him, but a generic humility which acknowledges in the universe a greater wisdom, power, righteousness than his own. That is formally acknowledged by our religion, but it is not practically acknowledged in our way of life, in our conduct or our thought. We think and feel and behave as if we were the best and wisest creatures in the universe, as if it existed only for us to make use of it; and in so far as we learn from it at all, we learn only to make use of it. That is our idea of knowledge and wisdom; more and more it is our idea of science; and as for philosophy, we pay no heed to it because, in its nature, it is not concerned with making use of things. In every way we betray the fact that we cannot listen humbly, because we do not believe there is anything to listen to. For a few of the devout God spoke long ago, but He is not speaking now. "The kings of modern thought are dumb," said Matthew Arnold; but that is because everything outside the mind of man is dumb; all must be dumb to those who will not listen. If we assume that there is no intelligence anywhere but in ourselves, we shall find none any-

Wilfulness and Wisdom

where else. There will be no meaning for us
in anything but our own actions; and they
will become more and more meaningless to us as
they become more and more wilful, until at last
we shall be to ourselves like squirrels in a cage,
or prisoners on a universal treadmill. Years
ago the war must have seemed a meaningless
treadmill to the Germans, but they cannot
escape from its consequences; they have done
and they must suffer. But will they learn from
their sufferings, shall we all learn, that doing
is not everything? Are we humbled enough
to listen to the wisdom of the ages, which tells
us that we can be wise only if we listen for a
wisdom that is not ours?

"The Magic Flute" ᴏ   ᴏ   ᴏ   ᴏ

WHEN *The Magic Flute* was produced by the already dying Mozart it had little success. At the first performance, it is said, when the applause was faint, the leader of the orchestra stole up to Mozart, who was conducting, and kissed his hand; and Mozart stroked him on the head. We may guess that the leader knew what the music meant and that Mozart knew that he knew. Neither could put it into words and it is not put into words in the libretto. But the libretto need not be an obstruction to the meaning of the music if only the audience will not ask themselves what the libretto means. After Mozart's death the opera was successful, no doubt because the audience had given up asking what the libretto meant and had learnt something of the meaning of the music.

There are worse librettos—librettos which have some clear unmusical meaning of their own beyond which the audience cannot penetrate to the meaning of the music, if it has

"The Magic Flute"

any. This libretto, apart from the music, is so nearly meaningless, it has so little coherence, that one can easily pass through it to the music. The author, Schickaneder, was Mozart's friend, and he had wit enough to understand the mood of Mozart. That mood does express itself in the plot and the incidents of the libretto, although in them it is empty of value or passion. Schickaneder, in fact, constructed a mere diagram to which Mozart gave life. The life is all in the music, but the diagram has its use, in that it supplies a shape, which we recognize, to the life of the music. The characters live in the music, but in the words they tell us something about themselves which enables us to understand their musical speech better. Papageno tells us that he is a bird-catcher and a child of nature. The words are labels, but through them we pass more quickly to an understanding of his song. Only we shall miss that understanding if we try to reach it through the words, if we look for the story of the opera in them. In the words the events of the opera have no connexion with each other. There is no reason why one should follow another. The logic of it is all in the music, for the music creates a world in which events happen naturally, in which one tune springs

out of another, or conflicts with it, like the
forces of nature or the thoughts and actions of
man. This world is the universe as Mozart
sees it; and the whole opera is an expression
of his peculiar faith. It is therefore a religious
work, though free from that meaningless and
timid solemnity which we associate with religion. Mozart, in this world, was like an
angel who could not but laugh, though without
any malice, at all the bitter earnestness of mankind. Even the wicked were only absurd to
him; they were naughty children whom, if one
had the spell, one could enchant into goodness.
And in *The Magic Flute* the spell works. It
works in the flute itself and in Papageno's lyre
when the wicked negro Monostatos threatens
him and Tamino with his ugly attendants.
Papageno has only to play a beautiful childish
tune on his lyre and the attendants all march
backwards to an absurd goose-step in time with
it. They are played off the stage; and the
music convinces one that they must yield to it.
So, we feel if we had had the music, we could
have made the Prussians march their goose-step
back to Potsdam; so we could play all solemn
perversity off the stage of life. If we had the
music—but there is solemn perversity in us too;
by reason of which we can hardly listen to the

music, much less play it, hardly listen to it or understand it even when Mozart makes it for us. For he had the secret of it; he was a philosopher who spoke in music and so simply that the world missed his wisdom and thought that he was just a beggar playing tunes in the street. A generation ago he was commonly said to be too tuney, as you might say that a flower was too flowery. People would no more consider him than they would consider the lilies of the field. They preferred Wagner in all his glory.

Even now you can enjoy *The Magic Flute* as a more than usually absurd musical comedy with easy, old-fashioned tunes. You can enjoy it anyway, if you are not solemn about it, as you can enjoy *Hamlet* for a bloody melodrama. But, like *Hamlet*, it has depths and depths of meaning beyond our full comprehension. Papageno is a pantomime figure, but he is also one of the greatest figures in the drama of the world. He is everyman, like Hamlet, if only we had the wit to recognize ourselves in him. Or rather he is that element in us which we all like and despise in others, but which we will never for one moment confess to in ourselves— the coward, the boaster, the liar, but the child of nature. He, because he knows himself for all of these, can find his home in Sarostro's paradise. He does not want Sarostro's high wisdom; what he does want is a Papagena, an Eve, a child of nature like himself; and she is given to him. He has the wit to recognize his mate, almost a bird like himself, and to them Mozart gives their bird-duet, so that, when they sing it, we feel that we might all sing it together. It is not above our capacity of understanding or delight. The angel has learnt our earthly tongue, but transformed it so that he makes a heaven of the earth, a heaven that is not too high or difficult for us, a wild-wood heaven, half-absurd, in which we can laugh as well as sing, and in which the angels will laugh at us and with us, laugh our silly sorrows into joy.

There is Mozart himself in Papageno, the faun domesticated and sweetened by centuries of Christian experience, yet still a faun and always ready to play a trick on human solemnity; and in this paradise which Mozart makes for us the faun has his place and a beauty not incongruous with it, like the imps and gargoyles of a Gothic church. At any moment the music will turn from sublimity into fun, and in a moment it can turn back to sublimity; and always the change seems natural.

"The Magic Flute"

It is like a great cathedral with High Mass and children playing hide-and-seek behind the pillars; and the Mass would not be itself without the children. That is the mind of Mozart which people have called frivolous, just because in his heaven there is room for everything except the vulgar glory of Solomon and cruelty and stupidity and ugliness. There never was anything in art more profound or beautiful than Sarostro's initiation music, but it is not, like the solemnities of the half-serious, incongruous with the twitterings of Papageno. Mozart's religion is so real that it seems to be not religion, but merely beauty, as real saints seem to be not good, but merely charming. And there are people to whom his beauty does not seem to be art, because it is just beauty; they think that he had the trick of it and could turn it on as he chose; they prefer the creaking of effort and egotism. His gifts are so purely gifts and so lavish that they seem to be cheap; and *The Magic Flute* is an absurdity which he wrote in a hurry to please the crowd.

We can hardly expect to see a satisfying performance of it on the stage of to-day, but we must be grateful for any performance, for the life of the music is in it. One can see from it what *The Magic Flute* might be. The music

is so sung, so played that it does transfigure
the peculiar theatrical hideousness of our time.
Tamino and Panina may look like figures out
of an Academy picture, as heroes and heroines
of opera always do. They may wear clothes
that belong to no world of reality or art,
clothes that suggest the posed and dressed-up
model. But the music mitigates even these,
and it helps every one to act, or rather to
forget what they have learnt about acting. It
evidently brings happiness and concord to those
who sing it, so that they seem to be taking
part in a religious act rather than in an act of
the theatre. One feels this most in the con-
certed music, when the same wind from paradise
seems to be blowing through all the singers
and they move to it like flowers, in spite of
their absurd clothes.

But what is needed for a satisfying performance is a world congruous to the eye as
well as to the ear; and for this we need a
break with all our theatrical conventions.
Sarostro, for instance, lives among Egyptian
scenery—very likely the architecture of his
temple was Egyptian at the first performance
—but, for all that, this Egyptian world does
not suit the music, and to us it suggests the
miracles of the Egyptian Hall. But there is

"The Magic Flute"

one world which would perfectly suit the music,
a world in which it could pass naturally from
absurdity to beauty, and in which all the figures
could be harmonious and yet distinct, and that
is the Chinese world as we know it in Chinese
art. For in that there is something fantastic
yet spiritual, something comic but beautiful, a
mixture of the childish and the sacred, which
might say to the eye what Mozart's music says
to the ear. Only in Chinese art could Papageno
be a saint; only in that world, which ranges
from the willow-pattern plate to the Rishi in
his mystical ecstasy in the wilderness, could the
soul of Mozart, with its laughter and its wisdom,
be at home. That too is the world in which
flowers and all animals are of equal import with
mankind; it is the world of dragons in which
the serpent of the first act would not seem to
be made of pasteboard, and in which all the
magic would not seem to be mere conjuring.
In that world one might have beautiful land-
scapes and beautiful figures to suit them.
There Sarostro would not be a stage magician,
but a priest; from Papageno and the lovers to
him would be only the change from Ming to
Sung, which would seem no change at all.
Chinese art, in fact, is the world of the magic
flute, the world where silver bells hang on

every flowering tree and the thickets are full of enchanted nightingales. It is the world of imps and monsters, and yet of impassioned contemplation, where the sage sits in a moonlit pavilion and smiles like a lover, and where the lovers smile like sages; where everything is to the eye what the music of Mozart is to the ear.

In the Chinese world we could be rid of all the drawling erotics of the modern theatre, we could give up the orchid for the lotus and the heavy egotism of Europe for the self-forgetful gaiety of the East. It may be only an ideal world, empty of the horrors of reality, but it is one which the art of China makes real to us and with which we are familiar in that art; and there is a smiling wisdom in it, there is a gaiety which comes from conquest rather than refusal of reality, just like the gaiety and wisdom of Mozart's music. He knew sorrow well, but would not luxuriate in it; he took the beauty of the universe more seriously than himself. To him wickedness was a matter of imps and monsters rather than of villains, and of imps and monsters that could be exorcized by music. He was the Orpheus of the world who might tame the beast in all of us if we would listen to him, the wandering minstrel whom the world left to

" The Magic Flute "

play out in the street. And yet his ultimate
seriousness and the last secret of his beauty is
pity, not for himself and his own little troubles,
but for the whole bitter earnestness of mortal
children. And in this pity he seems not to
weep for us, still less for himself, but to tell us
to dry our tears and be good, and listen to his
magic flute. That is what he would have told
the Prussians, after he had set them marching
the goose-step backwards. Even they would
not be the villains of a tragedy for him, but
only beasts to be tamed with his music until
they should be fit to sing their own bass part
in the last chorus of reconciliation. And this
pity of his sounds all through *The Magic Flute*
and gives to its beauty a thrill and a wonder
far beyond what any fleshly passion can give.
Sarostro is a priest, not a magician, because there
is in him the lovely wisdom of pity, because he
has a place in his paradise for Papageno, the
child of nature, where he shall be made happy
with his mate Papagena. There is a moment
when Papageno is about to hang himself
because there is no one to love him ; he will
hang himself in Sarostro's lonely paradise.
But there is a sly laughter in the music which
tells us that he will be interrupted with the
rope round his neck. And so he is, and

Papagena is given to him, and the paradise is no longer lonely ; and the two sing their part in the chorus of reconciliation at the end. And we are sure that the Queen of Night, and the ugly negro and all his goose-stepping attendants, are not punished. They have been naughty for no reason that anyone can discover, just like Prussians and other human beings ; and now the magic flute triumphs over their naughtiness, and the silver bells ring from every tree and the enchanted nightingales sing in all the thickets, and the sages and the lovers smile like children ; and the laughter passes naturally into the divine beauty of Mozart's religion, which is solemn because laughter and pity are reconciled in it, not rejected as profane.

Process or Person? ✍ ✍ ✍ ✍

NEARLY all war pictures in the past have been merely pictures that happened to represent war. Paolo Uccello's battle scenes are but pretexts for his peculiar version of the visible world. They might as well be still life for all the effect the subject has had upon his treatment of it. Leonardo, in his lost battle picture, was no doubt dramatic, and expressed in it his infinite curiosity; he has left notes about the manner in which fighting men and horses ought to be represented, but he had this detached curiosity about all things. Michelangelo's battle picture, also lost, expressed his interest in the nude in violent action, like his picture of the "Last Judgment." Titian's "Battle of Cadore," which we know from the copy of a fragment of it, was a landscape with figures in violent action. Tintoret's battle scenes are parade pictures. Those of Rubens are like his hunting scenes or his Bacchanals, expressions of his own overweening energy. In none of these, except perhaps in Leonardo's, was there implied any criticism of war, or any sense that it is an abnormal activity of man. The men who take part in it are just men fighting; they are not men seen differently because they are fighting, or in any way robbed of their humanity because of their inhuman business. As for Meissonier, he paints a battle scene just as if he were a second-rate Dutchman painting a *genre* picture; and most other modern military painters make merely a patriotic appeal. War to them also is a normal occupation; and they paint battle pictures as they might paint sporting pictures, because there is a public that likes them.

In Mr. Nevinson's war pictures there is expressed a modern sense of war as an abnormal occupation; and this sense shows itself in the very method of the artist. He was something of a Cubist before the war; but in these pictures he has found a new reason for being one; for his cubist method does express, in the most direct way, his sense that in war man behaves like a machine or part of a machine, that war is a process in which man is not treated as a human being but as an item in a great instrument of destruction, in which he ceases to be a person and is lost in a

Process or Person ?

process. The cubist method, with its repetition and sharp distinction of planes, expresses this sense of mechanical process better than any other way of representation. Perhaps it came into being to express the modern sense of process as the ultimate reality of all things, even of life and growth. This is the age of mechanism; and machines have affected even our view of the universe; we are overawed by our own knowledge and inventions. Samuel Butler imagined a future in which machines would come to life and make us their slaves; but it is not so much that machines have come to life as that we ourselves have lost the pride and sweetness of our humanity; not that the machines seem more and more like us, but that we seem more and more like the machines. Everywhere we see processes to which we are subject and of which our humanity is the result, though in the past we have harboured the delusion that our humanity was in some way independent of processes. Now that delusion is fading away from us; and it fades away most of all in war, where all humanity is evidently dominated by the struggle for life, and is but a part of it, as raindrops are part of a storm.

It is this sense of tyrannous process that Mr.

Nevinson expresses in his battle pictures, with, we suspect, a bitter feeling of resentment against it. His pictures look like a visible *reductio ad absurdum* of it all. That is how men look, he seems to say, when they are fighting in modern war; and, being men, they ought not to look so. That, at least, is the effect the pictures produce on us. They are a bitter satire on all the modern power of man and the uses to which he has put it. He has allowed it to make him its slave and to set him to a business which has no purpose whatever, which is as blind as the process of the universe seems to one who has no faith. This struggle for life might just as well be called a struggle for death. It is, in fact, merely a struggle between two machines intent on wrecking each other; and part of the machines are the bodies of men, which behave as if there were no souls in them, as if there were not even life, but merely energy; so that they collide and destroy each other like masses of matter in space. Nothing can be said of them except that they obey certain laws; we call their obedience discipline, but it is only the discipline of things subject to a process.

Now it is the sense of process, as the ultimate reality in the universe, which has produced war against the conscience of mankind, and even of many Germans. Conscience was powerless to prevent it because conscience had ceased to believe in its own power, had come to think of itself as a vain and inexplicable rebellion against the nature of things. This rebellion we call sentimentality, meaning thereby that it is really not even moral; for true morality would recognize the process to which the nature of man is subject, of which that nature is itself a part; and would cure man of his futile rebellions so that he should not suffer needlessly from them. It would cure man of pity, because it is through pity that he suffers. He is a machine, and, if he is a conscious machine, he should be conscious of the fact that he is one. Such is the belief that has been growing upon us for fifty years or more with many strange effects. It has not destroyed our sense of pity, but has confused and exasperated it. We pity and love still, but with desperation, not like Christians assured that these things are according to the order of the universe, but fearing that they are wilful exceptions to that order, costly luxuries that we indulge in at our own peril. We seem to ourselves lonely in our pity and love; the supreme process knows nothing of them; the God, who is love, does not exist.

In the past wars have happened with the consent of mankind; but this war did not happen so. Even in Germany there was something hysterical in the praise of war, as if it were the worship of an idol both hated and feared. We must praise war, the German worshippers of force seem to say, so that we may survive. We must forgo the past hopes of man so that we may find something real to hope for. We must habituate ourselves to the universe as it is, and break ourselves and all mankind in to the bitter truth. They praised war as we used in England to praise industry. Labour, we believed, when all the labour of the poor had been made joyless by the industrial revolution, was the result of the curse laid upon man by God. Therefore, man must labour without joy and never dream of happy work. And so now the very worshippers of war believe that it is a curse laid upon man by the nature of things. They may not believe in the fall of man, but they do believe that he can never rise, since he is himself part of a process which is always war; and, if he tries to escape from it, he will become extinct. So they exhort us to consent to that process even

Process or Person ?

with our conscience; the more completely we
consent to it, the more we shall succeed in it.
But all the while they are doing violence to our
natures and to their own. They try to think
like machines, like the slaves of a process; but
thought itself is inconsistent with their effort;
their very praises of the heroism of their
victims are inconsistent with it. There is
a gaping incongruity between the obsolete
German romanticism and the new German
atheism which exploited it, between their talk
about Siegfried and their talk about the
struggle for life. And there is the same
incongruity between the cubist effort to see the
visible world as a mechanical process and art
itself. The cubist seems to force himself with
a savage irony into this caricature of nature;
we have emptied reality of its content in our
thought and he will empty it of its content to
our eyes; that is not how we really see things,
but it is how we ought to see them if what
we believe about the nature of things is true.
This irony we find in Mr. Nevinson's pictures
of the war, whether it be a despairing irony or
the rebellion of an unshaken faith. He has
emptied man of his content, just as the
Prussian drill sergeant would empty him of his
content for the purposes of war; and only a

Prussian drill sergeant could consent to this version of man with any joy.

That, perhaps, is how we shall all come to see everything if we continue for some centuries to believe that process and not person is the ultimate reality. Emptying ourselves of all our content in thought, we shall at last empty ourselves of all content in reality; we shall become what now we fear we are, and our very senses will be obedient to our unfaith. For unfaith is the belief in process; and faith is the belief in person. It is the belief in process that makes men sacrifice other men in thousands to some idol; it is the belief in person that makes them refuse to sacrifice anyone but themselves; and they are afraid when they sacrifice others, but confident when they sacrifice themselves. Ultimately process has no value and can have no value for us. It is merely what exists or what we believe to exist, and our effort to value it is only the obsequiousness of the slave to the power that he fears. All our values come from the sense of person as more real than process. We will not do wrong to a man because he is a man; if he is to us only part of a process, we cannot value him and we can do what we will to him without any sense of wrong. All the old

Process or Person?

cruelties and iniquities of the world arose out
of a belief in process and a fear of it. It is
not a modern scientific discovery, but the
oldest and darkest superstition that has
oppressed the mind of man. To all religious
persecutors salvation was a process, like that
struggle for life which is the modern form of
the struggle for salvation to the superstitious.
And because salvation was a process human
beings were sacrificed to it. It did not matter
how they were tortured, provided this abstract
process was maintained. So it does not matter
now how they are slaughtered, provided the
abstract process of the struggle for life is maintained. To the German this war was part of a
process, the historical process of the triumph of
Germany, and it did not matter how many
Germans were killed in furthering it. If they
were all killed Germany would still have
asserted her faithless faith in process and
would have reduced it to a glorious absurdity.

So, if we fought for anything beyond ourselves, we fought for the belief in person as
against the belief in process. Indeed, it is the
chief glory of England, among her many follies
and crimes, that she has always believed in
person rather than in process; and that is
what we mean when we say that we refuse to

sacrifice facts to theories. Men themselves are to us facts, and we distrust theories that empty them of content. If we act like brutes, we would rather do so because the brute has mastered us for the moment than because we believe that humanity is inconsistent with the process that dominates the world. We ourselves had rather be inconsistent than empty ourselves of all reality for the sake of a theory. And there is an intellectual as well as a moral basis to this inconsistency of ours. For if you believe that person, not process, is the ultimate reality, you must offer some defiance to the material facts of life. There is evidently a conflict between person and process; and in that conflict the process, which you perceive with your intelligence, will be less real to you than the person of whom you are aware with all your faculties. So you will trust in this union of all the faculties rather than in the exercise of the pure intelligence; for to you the pure intelligence will be part of the person and will share in the person's universal imperfection. In fact it will not be pure intelligence at all, but rather a faculty that may be obsequious to all the lower passions. Nothing will free you from them, except the respect for persons, except, in fact, loving your neighbour as yourself. There is no way to consistency but through that, and no way to the exercise of the pure intelligence. Never sacrifice a person to a process and you will never sacrifice a person to your own lower passions. But, if you believe in process rather than in person, you will see your passions as part of the process and glorify them when you think you are glorifying the nature of the universe.

Cubism and all those new methods of art which subject facts to the tyranny of a process may be good satire, but they will never, I think, produce an independent beauty of their own. Like all satire, they are parasitic upon past art, negative and rebellious. They tell us what the universe may look like to us if we lose all faith in ourselves and each other ; and, when they are the result of a desperate effort to see the universe so, they are unconscious satire. The complete, convinced cubist reduces his own method, his own beliefs, his own state of mind, to an absurdity. The more sincere he is, the more complete is the reduction. For he, rejecting all that has been the subject-matter of painting in the past, all the human values and the complexes of association which have invested the visible world with beauty for men, proves to us in his tortured diagrams

that he has found nothing to take their place,
He gives us a *Chimæra bombinans in vacuo*, that
vacuum which the universe is to the human
spirit when it denies itself. He tries to make
art, having cut himself off from all the experience and belief that produce art. For art
springs always out of a supreme value for the
personal and is an expression of that value. It
is an effort, no matter in what medium, to
find the personal in all things, to see trees as
men walking ; and the new abstract methods
in painting reverse this process, they empty
all things, even men, of personality and subject
them to a process invented by the artist, which
expresses, if it expresses anything, his own loss
of personal values and nothing else. The
result may be ingenious, it may still have a
kind of beauty remembered from the great
design of past art ; but it will lead nowhere,
since it is cut off from the very experience, the
passionate personal interest in people and
things, which gave design to the great art of
the past. It is at best satirical, at worst
parasitic, using up all devices of design and
turning from one to another in a restless ennui
which of itself can give no enrichment. It
may have its uses, since it insists upon the
supreme importance of design and provides a

new method for the expression of three dimensions; but this method will be barren unless those who practise it enrich it with their own observation and delight. Already some of them seem to be weary of the barrenness of pure abstraction; they see that any fool can hide his own commonplace in cubism as an ostrich hides its head in the sand; but we would rather have honest chocolate-box ladies than the kaleidoscopic but betraying chocolate-box fragments of the futurist.

The Artist and the Tradesman ✍ ✍

THE Exhibition of the Arts and Crafts at Burlington House was an acknowledgment of the fact that there are other arts besides those of painting, sculpture, and architecture, or rather perhaps that the arts subsidiary to architecture are arts and not merely commercial activities. Burlington House would protest, of course, that it is not a shop; but now at last objects are to be shown in it which the great mass of the public expects to see only in shops and expects to be produced merely to sell. We remember how Lord Grimthorpe called Morris a poetic upholsterer. He meant there was something incongruous in the combination of an upholsterer and a poet; he would have seen nothing incongruous in the combination of a poet and a painter, because he would have called a painter an artist; but an upholsterer was to him merely a tradesman, and tradesmen are not expected to write poetry. Their business is to sell things and to make objects for sale.

The Artist and the Tradesman

In that respect he thought like the mass of the public now. For them the painter has some prestige, because he is supposed not to be a tradesman, not to paint his pictures merely so that he may sell them. He has to live by his art, of course, but he practises it also because he enjoys it; and, if he is an artist, he will not paint bad pictures merely because they are what the public wants. But it is the business of those who make furniture and such things to produce what the public wants. No one would blame them for producing what they do not like themselves, any more than one would blame a pill-maker for producing pills that he would not swallow himself. The pill-maker and the furniture-maker are both tradesmen producing objects in answer to a demand. They have no prestige and no conscience is expected of them.

Now in Italy in the fifteenth century this distinction between the artist and the tradesman did not exist. The painter was a tradesman; he kept a shop and he had none of that peculiar prestige which he possesses now. But of the tradesman more was expected than is expected now; for instance, good workmanship and material were expected of him and also good design. He did not produce articles merely to sell, whether they were pictures or wedding-chests or jewelry or pots and pans. He made all these other things just as he made pictures, with some pleasure and conscience in his own work; and it was the best craftsman who became a painter or sculptor, merely because those were the most difficult crafts. Now it is the gentleman with artistic faculty who becomes a painter; the poor man, however much of that faculty he possesses, remains a workman without any artistic prestige and without any temptation to consider the quality of his work or to take any pleasure in it. This is a commonplace, no doubt; but it remains a fact, however often it may have been repeated, and a social fact with a constant evil effect upon all the arts. Because the painter is supposed to be an artist and nothing else and the craftsman a tradesman and nothing else, we do not expect the virtues of the craftsman from the painter nor the virtues of the artist from the craftsman. For us there is nothing but mystery in the work of the artist and no mystery at all in the work of the craftsman. The painter can be as silly as he likes, and we do not laugh at him, if we are persons of culture, because his art is a sacred mystery. But, as for the crafts-

The Artist and the Tradesman

man, there is nothing sacred about his work. It is sold in a shop and made to be sold; and all we expect of it is that it shall be in the fashion, which means that it shall be what the commercial traveller thinks he can sell. There are, of course, a few craftsman who are thought of as artists, and their work at once becomes a sacred mystery, like pictures. They too have a right to be as silly as they like; and some people will buy their work, however silly it may be, as they would buy pictures—that is to say, for the good of their souls and not because they like it.

How are we to get rid of this distinction we have made between the artist and the tradesman? How are we to recover for the artist the virtues of the craftsman and for the craftsman the virtues of the artist? At present we get from neither what we really like. Art remains to us a painful mystery; most of us would define it, if we were honest, as that which human beings buy because they do not like it. While, as for objects of use, they are bought mainly because they are sold; they are forced upon us as a conjurer forces a card. We think we like them while they remain the fashion; but soon they are like women's clothes of two years ago, if they last

long enough to be outmoded. It is vain for us
to reproach either the artist or the tradesman.
The fault is in ourselves ; we have as a whole
society yielded to the most subtle temptation
of Satan. We have lost the power of knowing what we like—that is to say, the power
of loving. We value nothing for itself, but
everything for its associations. The man of
culture buys a picture, not because he likes it,
but because he thinks it is art ; at most what
he enjoys is not the picture itself but the
thought that he is cultured enough to enjoy it.
That thought comes between him and the
picture, and makes it impossible for him to experience the picture at all. And so he is
ready to accept anything that the painter
chooses to give him, if only he believes the
painter to be a real artist. This is bad for the
painter, who has every temptation to become
a charlatan, and to think of his art as a sacred
mystery which no one can understand but
himself and a few other painters of his own
sect. But in this matter the man of culture
is just like the vulgar herd, as he would call
them. Their attitude to the arts of use is the
same as his attitude to pictures. They do not
buy furniture or china because they like them,
but because the shopman persuades them that

The Artist and the Tradesman

what they buy is the fashion. Or perhaps they recognize it themselves as the fashion and therefore instantly believe that they like it. In both cases the buyer is hypnotized; he has lost the faculty of finding out for himself what he really likes, and his mind, being empty of real affection, is open to the seven devils of suggestion. He cannot enjoy directly any beautiful thing, all he can enjoy is the belief that he is enjoying it; and he can harbour this belief about any nonsense or trash.

It is a very curious disease that has become endemic in the whole of Europe. People impute it to machinery, but unjustly. There are objects made by machinery, such as motor-cars, which have real beauty of design; and people do genuinely and unconsciously enjoy this beauty, just because they never think of it as beauty. They like the look of a car because they can see that it is well made for its purpose. If only they would like the look of any object of use for the same reason, the arts of use would once again begin to flourish among us. But when once we ask ourselves whether any thing is beautiful, we become incapable of knowing our real feelings about it. Any tradesman or artist can persuade us that we think it beautiful when we do nothing of the kind. We are all like the crowd who admired the Emperor's clothes; and there is no child to tell us that the Emperor has no clothes on at all. We are not so with human beings; we cannot be persuaded that we like a man when really we dislike him; if we could, our whole society would soon dissolve in a moral anarchy. But with regard to the works of man, or that part of them which is supposed to aim at beauty, we are in a state of æsthetic anarchy, because there is a whole vast conspiracy, itself unconscious for the most part, to persuade us that we like what no human being out of a madhouse could like.

So the real problem for us is to discover, not merely in pictures, but in all things that are supposed to have beauty, what we really do like. And we can best do that, perhaps, if we dismiss the notions of art and beauty for a time from our minds; not because art and beauty do not exist, but because our notions of them are wrong and misleading. The very words intimidate us, as people used to be intimidated by the jargon of pietistic religion, so that they would believe that a very unpleasant person was a saint. When once we look for beauty in anything, we look no longer for good design, good workmanship, or good

The Artist and the Tradesman

material. It is because we do not look for
beauty in motor-cars that we enjoy the excellence of their design, workmanship, and
material, which is beauty, if only we knew it.
Beauty, in fact, is a symptom of success in
things made by man, not of success in selling,
but of success in making. If an object made
by man gives us pleasure in itself, then it has
beauty; if we got pleasure only from the belief
that in it we are enjoying what we ought to
enjoy, then very likely it is as naked of beauty
as the Emperor was of clothes. The great
mass of people now have a belief that ornament is necessarily beauty, that, without it,
nothing can be beautiful. But ornament is
often only added ugliness, like a wen on a
man's face. It is always added ugliness when
it is machine-made, and when it is put on to
hide cheapness of material and faults of design
and workmanship. Unfortunately, it does hide
these things from us; we accept ornament as
a substitute for that beauty which can only
come of good design, material, and workmanship; and we do not recognize these things
when we see them, except in objects like
motor-cars, which we prefer plain because we
do unconsciously enjoy their real beauty.

So, in the matter of ornament, we need to

make a self-denying ordinance; not because
ornament is necessarily bad—it is the natural
expression of the artist's superfluous energy
and delight—but because we ourselves cannot
be trusted with ornament, as a drunkard cannot
be trusted with strong drink. We must learn
to see things plain before we can see them at
all, or enjoy them for their own real qualities
and not for what we think we see in them. A
man whose taste is for bad poetry can only
improve it by reading good, plain prose. He
must become rational before he can enjoy the
real beauties of literature. And so we need
to become rational before we can enjoy art,
whether in pictures or in objects of use. The
unreason of our painting has the same cause
as the unreason of our objects of use; and the
cause is in us, not in the artist. We think of
taste as something in its nature irrational. It
is no more so than conscience is. Indeed, there
is conscience in all good taste as in all the
good workmanship that pleases it. But where
the public has not this conscience, the artist
will not possess it either. At best he will have
only what he calls his artistic conscience—that
is to say, a determination to follow his own
whims rather than the taste of the public.
But where the public knows what it likes, and

The Artist and the Tradesman

the artist makes what he likes, there is more
than a chance that both will like the same
thing, as they have in the great ages of art.
For a real liking must be a liking for something good.   It is Satan who persuades us
that we like what is bad by filling our mind
with sham likings, which are always really the
expression of our egotism disguised.

Professionalism in Art ✄ ✄ ✄

PROFESSIONALISM is a dull, ugly word ; but it means dull, ugly things, a perversion of the higher activities of man, of art, literature, religion, philosophy ; and a perversion to which we are all apt to be blind. We know that in these activities specialization is a condition of excellence. As Keats said to Shelley, in art it is necessary to serve both God and Mammon ; and as Samuel Butler said, "That is not easy, but then nothing that is really worth doing ever is easy." The poet may be born, not made ; but no man can start writing poetry as if it had never been written before. In every art there is a medium, and the poet, like all other artists, learns from the poets of the past how to use his medium. Often he does this unconsciously by reading them for delight. He first becomes a poet because he loves the poetry of others. And the painter becomes a painter because he loves the pictures of others. Each of them is apt to begin—

> As if his whole vocation
> Were endless imitation.

Professionalism in Art

So the artist insists to himself upon the value of hard work. He is impatient of all the talk about inspiration; for he knows that, though nothing can be done without it, it comes only with command of the medium. And this command, like all craftsmanship, is traditional, handed down from one generation to another. Any kind of expression in this imperfect world is as difficult as virtue itself. For expression, like virtue, is a kind of transcendence. In it the natural man rises above his animal functions, above living so that he may continue to live; he triumphs over those animal functions which hold him down to the earth as incessantly as the attraction of gravity itself. But, like the airman, he can triumph only by material means, and by means gradually perfected in the practice of others. Yet there is always this difference, that in mechanics anyone can learn to make use of an invention; but in the higher activities, invention, if it becomes mechanical, destroys the activity itself, even in the original inventor. The medium is always a medium, not merely a material; and if it becomes merely a material to be manipulated, it ceases to be a medium.

Now professionalism is the result of a false analogy between mechanical invention and the higher activities. It happens whenever the medium is regarded merely as material to be manipulated, when the artist thinks that he can learn to fly by mastering some other artist's machine, when his art is to him a matter of invention gradually perfected and necessarily progressing through the advance of knowledge and skill. One often finds this false analogy in books about the history of the arts, especially of painting and music. It is assumed, for instance, that Italian painting progressed mechanically from Giotto to Titian, that Titian had a greater power of expression than Giotto because he had command of a number of inventions in anatomy and perspective and the like that were unknown to Giotto. So we have histories of the development of the symphony, in which Haydn, Mozart, Beethoven are treated as if they were mechanical inventors each profiting by the discoveries of his predecessors. Beethoven was the greatest of the three because he had the luck to be born last, and Beethoven's earliest symphonies are necessarily better than Mozart's latest because they were composed later. But in such histories there always comes a point at which artists cease to profit by the inventions of their predecessors. After Michelangelo, perhaps after Beethoven, is the decadence. Then sud-

denly there is talk of inspiration, or the lack
of it.   Mere imitators appear, and the historian
who reviles them does not see that they have
only practised, and refuted, his theory of art.
They also have had the luck to be born later;
but it has been bad luck, not good, for
them, because to them their art has been all
a matter of mechanical invention, of professionalism.

The worst of it is that the greatest artists
are apt themselves to fall in love with their
own inventions, not to see that they are
mechanical inventions because they themselves have discovered them.   Michelangelo
in his " Last Judgment " is very professional;
Titian was professional through all his middle
age; Tintoret was professional whenever he
was bored with his work, which happened
often; Shakespeare, whenever he was lazy,
which was not seldom.   Beethoven, we now begin to see, could be very earnestly professional;
and as for Milton—consider this end of the
last speech of Manoah, in *Samson Agonistes*,
where we expect a simple cadence :—

> The virgins also shall on feastful days
> Visit his tomb with flowers, only bewailing
> His lot unfortunate in nuptial choice,
> From whence captivity and loss of eyes.

Milton was tempted into the jargon of these last two lines, which are like a bad translation of a Greek play, by professionalism He was trying to make his poetry as much unlike ordinary speech as he could; he was for the moment a slave to a tradition, and none the less a slave because it was the tradition of his own past.

Professionalism is a device for making expression easy; and it is one used by the greatest artists sometimes because their business is to be always expressing themselves, and even they have not always something to express. But expression is so difficult, even for those who have something to express, that they must be always practising it if they are ever to succeed in it. Wordsworth, for instance, was a professed enemy of professionalism in poetry; yet he, too, was for ever writing verses. It was a hobby with him as well as an art; and his professionalism was merely less accomplished than that of Milton or Spenser :—

> Fair Ellen Irwin, when she sate
> Upon the Braes of Kirtle,
> Was lovely as a Grecian maid
> Adorned with wreaths of myrtle.

Why adorned with wreaths of myrtle? Wordsworth himself tells us. His subject had already been treated in Scotch poems " in simple ballad

strain," so, he says, " at the outset I threw out
a classical image to prepare the reader for the
style in which I meant to treat the story, and
so to preclude all comparison." No one, whose
object was just to tell the story, would compare
Ellen with a Grecian maid and her wreaths of
myrtle; but Wordsworth must do so to show
us how he means to tell it, and, as he forgets
to mention, so that he may rhyme with Kirtle.
That is all professionalism, all a device for
making expression easy, practised by a great
poet because at the moment he had nothing to
express. But art is always difficult and cannot
be made easy by this means. We need not
take a malicious pleasure in such lapses of the
great poet; but it is well to know when Homer
nods, even though he uses all his craft to pretend that he is wide awake. Criticism may
have a negative as well as a positive value. It
may set us on our guard against professionalism even in the greatest artists, and most of
all in them. For it is they who begin professionalism and, with the mere momentum of
their vitality, make it attractive. Because
they are great men and really accomplished,
they can say nothing with a grand air; and
these grand nothings of theirs allure us just
because they are nothings and make no

demands upon our intelligence. That is art indeed, we cry; and we intoxicate ourselves with it because it is merely art. "The quality of mercy is not strained" is far more popular than Lear's speech, "No, no, no! Come, let's away to prison," because it is professional rhetoric; it is what Shakespeare could write at any moment, whereas the speech of Lear is what Lear said at one particular moment. The contrast between the two is the contrast well put in the epigram about Barry and Garrick in their renderings of King Lear:—

A king, aye, every inch a king, such Barry doth appear.
But Garrick's quite another thing; he's every inch King Lear.

We admire the great artist when he is every inch a king more than when he has lost his kingship in his passion.

He no doubt knows the difference well enough. But he wishes to do everything well, he has a natural human delight in his own accomplishment; and a job to finish. Shakespeare, Michelangelo, Beethoven were not slaves to their own professionalism; no doubt they could laugh at it themselves. But there is always a danger that we shall be enslaved by it; and it is the business of criticism to free us

Professionalism in Art

from that slavery, to make us aware of this last infirmity of great artists. We are on our guard easily enough against a professionalism that is out of fashion. The Wagnerian of a generation ago could sneer at the professionalism of Mozart; but the professionalism of Wagner seemed to him to be inspiration made constant and certain by a new musical invention. We know now only too well, from Wagner's imitators, that he did not invent a new method of tapping inspiration; we ought to know that no one can do that. The more complete the method the more tiresome it becomes, even as practised by the inventor.

Decadence in art is always caused by professionalism, which makes the technique of art too difficult, and so destroys the artist's energy and joy in his practice of it. Teachers of the arts are always inclined to insist on their difficulty and to set hard tasks to their pupils for the sake of their hardness; and often the pupil stays too long learning until he thinks that anything which is difficult to do must therefore be worth doing. This notion also overawes the general public so that they value what looks to them difficult; but in art that which seems difficult to us fails with us, we are aware of the difficulty, not of the art. The greater

the work of art the easier it seems to us. We
feel that we could have done it ourselves if only
we had had the luck to hit upon that way of
doing it; indeed, where our æsthetic experience
of it is complete, we feel as if we were doing it
ourselves; our minds jump with the artist's
mind; we are for the moment the artist himself in his very act of creation. But we are
always apt to undervalue this true and complete
æsthetic experience, because it seems so easy
and simple, and we mistake for it a painful
sense of the artist's skill, of his professional
accomplishment. So we demand of artists
that they shall impress us with their accomplishment; we have not had our money's worth
unless we feel that we could not possibly do
ourselves what they have done. No doubt,
when the *Songs of Innocence* were first published, anyone who did happen to read them
thought them doggerel. Blake in a moment
had freed himself from all the professionalism
of the followers of Pope, and even now they
make poetry seem an easy art to us, until we
try to write songs of innocence ourselves :—

When the voices of children are heard on the green,
  And laughing is heard on the hill,
My heart is at rest within my breast,
  And everything else is still.

Professionalism in Art

"Then come home, my children, the sun is gone
    down,
  And the dews of night arise;
Come, come, leave off play, and let us away,
  Till the morning appears in the skies."

We call it artless, with still a hint of deprecia-
tion in the word, or at least of wonder that we
should be so moved by such simple means.
It is a kind of cottage-poetry, and has that
beauty which in a cottage moves us more than
all the art of palaces. But we never learn
the lesson of that beauty because it seems to
us so easily won; and so our arts are always
threatened by the decadence of professionalism.
But poetry in England has been a living art
so long because it has had the power of freeing
itself from professionalism and choosing the
better path with Mary and with Ruth. The
value of the Romantic movement lay, not in
its escape to the wonders of the past, but in its
escape from professionalism and all its self-
imposed and easy difficulties. For it is much
easier to write professional verses in any style
than to write songs of innocence; and that is
why professionalism in all the arts tempts all
kinds of artists. Anyone can achieve it who
has the mind. It is a substitute for expression,
as mere duty is a substitute for virtue. But, as

a forbidding sense of duty makes virtue itself seem unattractive, so professionalism destroys men's natural delight in the arts. Like the artist himself, his public becomes anxious, perverse, exacting; afraid lest it shall admire the wrong thing, because it has lost the immediate sense of the right thing. Just as it expects art to be difficult, so it expects its own pleasure in art to be difficult; and thus we have attained to our present notion about art which is like the Puritan notion about virtue, that it is what no human being could possibly enjoy by nature. And if we do enjoy it, "like a meadow gale in spring," it cannot be good art.

But in painting as in poetry, all the new movements of value are escapes from professionalism; and they begin by shocking the public because they seem to make the art too easy. Dickens was horrified by an early work of Millais; Ruskin was enraged by a nocturne of Whistler. He said it was cockney impudence because it lacked the professionalism he expected. Artists and critics alike are always binding burdens on the arts; and they are always angry with the artist who cuts the burden off his back. They think he is merely shirking difficulties. But the difficulty of expression is so much greater than the self-imposed diffi-

Professionalism in Art

culties of mere professionalism that any man
who is afraid of difficulties will try to be a professional rather than an artist.

In art there is always humility, in professionalism pride. And it is this pride that
makes art more ugly and tiresome than any
other work of man. Nothing is stranger in
human nature than the tyranny of boredom
it will endure in the pursuit of art; and the
more bored men are, the more they are convinced
of artistic salvation. Our museums are cum-
bered with monstrous monuments of past professionalism; our bookshelves groan with them.
Always we are trying to like things because
they seem to us very well done; never do we
dare to say to ourselves: It may be well done,
but it were better if it were not done at all;
and the artist is still to us a dog walking on his
hind legs, a performer whose merit lies in the
unnatural difficulty of his performance.

Waste or Creation? ∞ ∞ ∞ ∞

THE William Morris Celebration was not so irrelevant to these times as it may seem. Morris was always foretelling a catastrophe to our society, and it has come. That commercial system of ours, which seems to so many part of the order of Nature, was to him as evil and unnatural as slavery. His quarrel with it was not political, but human; it was the quarrel not of the oppressed, for he was not the man to be oppressed in any society, but of the workman. He was sure that a society which encouraged bad work and discouraged good must in some way or other come to a bad end; and he would have seen in this war the end that he predicted. Whatever its result, there must be a change in the order of our society, whether it sinks through incessant wars, national and commercial, into barbarism or is shocked into an effort to attain to civilization. There were particular sayings of Morris's to which no one at the time paid much heed. They seemed mere grumblings against what must be. He was, for instance, always crying out against our waste of labour. If only all men did work that was worth doing—

Think what a change that would make in the world! I tell you I feel dazed at the thought of the immensity of the work which is undergone for the making of useless things. It would be an instructive day's work, for any one of us who is strong enough, to walk through two or three of the principal streets of London on a weekday, and take accurate note of everything in the shop windows which is embarrassing or superfluous to the daily life of a serious man. Nay, the most of these things no one, serious or unserious, wants at all; only a foolish habit makes even the lightest-minded of us suppose that he wants them; and to many people, even of those who buy them, they are obvious encumbrances to real work, thought, and pleasure.

At the time most people said that this waste of labour was all a matter of demand and supply, and thought no more about it; some said that it was good for trade. Very few saw, with Morris, that demand for such things is something willed and something that ought not to be willed.

But then it was generally believed that we could afford this waste of labour; and so it went on until, after a year or two of war, we found that we could not afford it. Then even the most ignorant and thoughtless learned, from facts, not from books, certain lessons of political economy. They learned that, in war-time at least, a nation that wastes its labour will be overcome by one that does not. At once the common will was set against the waste of labour; and, what would have seemed strangest of all forty years ago, the Government, with the consent of the people, set to work to stop the waste of labour, and did to a great extent succeed in stopping it. When people thought in terms of munitions, instead of in terms of general well-being, they saw that the waste of labour must be, and could be, stopped. They talked no longer about the laws of supply and demand, but about munitions. Those who had made trash must be set to make munitions, or to fight, or in some way to second the Army. Those who still were ready to waste labour on trash for themselves were no longer obeying the laws of supply and demand; they were diverting 'labour from its proper task; they were un-patriotic, they were helping the Germans. Money, in fact, had no longer the right to an absolute command over labour. A man, before he spent a sovereign, must ask himself whether he was spending it for the good of the nation; and if he did not ask himself that, the Government would ask it for him.

Waste or Creation ?

So much the war taught us, for purposes of war. But Morris many years ago tried to teach it for purposes of peace. When he wrote those words which we have quoted, he was not talking politics but ordinary common sense. He was not even talking art, but rather economics; and he was talking it not to any vague abstraction called the community, but to each individual human being. At that time every one thought of economics as something which concerned society or the universe. It was, so to speak, a natural science; it observed phenomena as if they were in the heavens; and stated laws about them, laws not human but natural. Perhaps it was the greatest achievement of Morris in the way of thought that he saw economics, even more clearly than Ruskin, as a matter not of natural laws, but of conscience and duty. He did not talk about economics at all, but about the waste of labour, just as we talk about it now. The only difference is that he saw it to be one of the chief causes of poverty in time of peace, whereas we see it as a hindrance to victory in time of war. We have, for war purposes, acquired the conscience that he wished us to acquire for all purposes. The question is whether we shall keep it in peace.

Upon that depends the question how soon

we shall recover from the war. For there is
no doubt that we shall not be able to afford
our former waste of labour; and, if we persist
in it, we shall be bankrupt as a society. It
may be said that we shall not have the money,
the power, to waste labour. But we shall certainly have some superfluous energy, more and
more, it is to be hoped, as time goes on; and
our future recovery will depend upon the use
we make of this superfluous energy. We can
waste it, as we wasted it before the war; or we
can keep the conscience we have acquired in
war and ask ourselves in peace, with every
penny we spend, whether we are wasting
labour. It is true that what may be waste to
one will not be waste to another; but in that
matter every one must obey his own conscience.
The important thing is that every one should
have a conscience and obey it. There will be
plenty of people to tell us that no one can
define waste of labour. No one can define sin;
but each man has his own conscience on that
point and lives well or ill as he obeys it or dis-
obeys it. Besides, there are many things, all
the trash that Morris speaks about in the shop
windows, that every one knows to be waste.
We need not trouble ourselves about the fact
that art will seem waste to the philistine and
not to the artist. We must allow for differ-

ences on that point as on most others. Some
things that might have been waste to Samuel
Smiles would have been to Morris a symptom
of well-being. But he knew, and often said,
that we cannot have the beauty which was to
him a symptom of well-being unless we end the
waste of labour on trash. Of luxury he said :—

By those who know of nothing better it has
even been taken for art, the divine solace of
human labour, the romance of each day's hard
practice of the difficult art of living. But I
say, art cannot live beside it nor self-respect in
any class of life. Effeminacy and brutality are
its companions on the right hand and the left.

There is, we have all discovered now, only a
certain amount of labour in the country, in the
world. Even the most ignorant are aware at
last that money does not create labour but
only commands it, and may command it to do
what will or will not benefit us all. We were,
for the purposes of the war, much more of a
fellowship than we had ever been before. We
acknowledged a duty to each other, the duty
of commanding labour to the common good.
We asked with every sovereign we spent
whether it would help or hinder us in the war.
Morris would have us ask also whether it will
help or hinder us in the advance towards a
general happiness.

And he put a further question, which in time of war unfortunately we could not put, a question not only about the work but about the workman. Are we, with our money, forcing him to work that is for him worth doing; are we, to use an old phrase, considering the good of his soul? Morris insisted on our duty to the workman more even than on our duty to society. He saw that where great masses of men do work that they know to be futile there must be a low standard of work and incessant discontent. The workman may not even know the cause of his discontent. He may think he is angry with the rich because they are rich; but the real source of his anger is the work that they set him to do with their riches. And no class war, no redistribution of wealth, will end that discontent if the same waste of labour continues. Double the wages of every workman in the country, and if he spends the increase on trash no one will be any better off in mind or body. There will still be poverty and still discontent, with the work if not with the wages.

The problem for us, for every modern society now, is not so much to redistribute wealth; that at best can be only a means to an end; but to use our superfluous energy to the best purpose, no longer to waste it piecemeal. That problem we solved, to a great extent, in war. We have to solve it also in peace if the peace is to be worth having and is not to lead to further wars at home or abroad. The war itself has given us a great opportunity. It has opened our eyes, if only we do not shut them again. It has taught every one in the country the most important of all lessons in political economy which the books often seem to conceal. And, better still, it has taught us that in economics we can exercise our own wills, that they concern each individual man and woman as much as morals; that they are morals, and not abstract mathematics; that we have the same duty towards the country, towards mankind, that we have to our own families. The proverb, Waste not, want not, does not apply merely to each private income. We have accounts to settle not only with our bankers, but with the community. It will thrive or not according as we are thrifty or thriftless; and our thrift depends upon how we spend our income, not merely on how much we spend of it. For all that part of it which we do not spend on necessaries is the superfluous energy of mankind, and we determine how it shall be exercised; each individual determines that, not an abstraction called society.

One may present the thrift of labour as a

matter of duty to society. But Morris saw that it was more than that; and he lit it with the sunlight of the warmer virtues. It is not merely society that we have to consider, or the direction of its superfluous energy. It is also the happiness, the life, of actual men and women. We shall not cease to waste work until we think always of the worker behind it, until we see that it is our duty, if with our money we have command over him, to set him to work worth doing. Capital now is to most of those who own it a means of earning interest. We should think of it as creative, as the power which may make the wilderness blossom like the rose and change the slum into a home for men and women; and, better still, as the power that may train and set men to do work that will satisfy their souls, so that they shall work for the work's sake and not only for the wages. Until capital becomes so creative in the hands of those who own it there will always be a struggle for the possession of it; and to those who do possess it it will bring merely super-fluities and not happiness. If it becomes creative, no one will mind much who possesses it. The class war will be ended by a league of classes, their aim not merely peace, but those things which make men resolve not to spoil peace with war.

Waste or Creation?

We shall be told that this is a dream, as we are always told that the ending of war is a dream. "So long as human nature is what it is there will always be war." Those who talk thus think of human nature as something not ourselves making for unrighteousness. It is not their own nature. They know that they themselves do not wish for war; but, looking at mankind in the mass and leaving themselves out of that mass, they see it governed by some force that is not really human nature, but merely nature "red in tooth and claw," a process become a malignant goddess, who forces mankind to act contrary to their own desires, contrary even to their own interests. She has taken the place for us of the old original sin; and the belief in her is far more primitive than the belief in original sin. She is in fact but a modern name for all the malignant idols that savages have worshipped with sacrifices of blood and tears that they did not wish to make. It is strange that, priding ourselves as we do on our modern scepticism which has taught us to disbelieve in the miracle of the Gadarene swine, we yet have not dared to affirm the plain fact that this nature, this human nature, does not exist. There is no force, no process, whether within us or outside us, that compels us to act contrary to our desires and our interests.

141

There is nothing but fear; and fear can be
conquered, as by individuals, so by the collec-
tive will of man. It is fear that produces war,
the fear that other men are not like ourselves,
that they are hostile animals governed utterly
by the instinct of self-preservation.

So it is fear that produces the class war and
the belief that it must always continue. It is
our own fears that cut us off from happiness
by making us despair of it. The man who has
capital sees it as a means of protecting himself
and his children from poverty; it is to him a
negative, defensive thing, at best the safeguard
of a negative, defensive happiness. So others
see it as something which he has and they have
not, something they would like to snatch from
him if they could. But if he saw capital as a
creative thing, like the powers of the mind,
like the genius of the artist, then it would be
to him a means of positive happiness both for
himself and for others. He would say to himself, not How can I protect myself with this
against the tyranny of the struggle for life?
not How can I invest this? but What can I do
with this? He would see it as Michelangelo
saw the marble when he looked for the shape
within it. And then he would rise above the
conception of mere duty as something we do
against our own wills, or of virtue as a luxury

of the spirit to which we escape in our little leisure from the struggle for life. Virtue, duty, would be for him life itself; in creation he would attain to that harmony of duty and pleasure which is happiness.

If only we could see that the superfluous energy of mankind is something out of which to make the happiness of mankind we should find our own happiness in the making of it. There is still for us a gulf between doing good to others and the delight of the artist, the craftsman, in his work. The artist is one kind of man and the philanthropist another; the artist is a selfish person whom we like, and the philanthropist an unselfish person whom we do not like. What we need is to fuse them in our use of capital, in our exercise of the superfluous energy of mankind. There are single powerful capitalists who know this joy of creation, who are benevolent despots, and yet are suspect to the poor because of their great power. But it never enters the head of the smaller investor that he, too, might create instead of merely investing; that, instead of being a shareholder in a limited liability company, he might be one of a creative fellowship, not merely earning dividends but transforming cities, exalting things of use into things of beauty, giving to himself and to mankind work worth doing for

its own sake, work in which all the obsolete
conflicts of rich and poor could be forgotten in
a commonwealth.   That is the vision of peace
which our sacrifices in the war may earn for us.
We have learned sacrifice and the joy of it;
but, so far, only so that we may overcome an
enemy of our own kind.   There remains to be
overcome, by a sacrifice more joyful and with
far greater rewards, this other old enemy not
of our own kind, the enemy we call nature or
human nature, the enemy that is so powerful
merely because we dare not believe that she
does not exist.